COOKING WITH PETA

GREAT VEGAN RECIPES
FOR A COMPASSIONATE KITCHEN

EDITED BY
PEOPLE FOR THE
ETHICAL TREATMENT OF ANIMALS

Book Publishing Company
Summertown, Tennessee

Front cover art and design: Peter Max
Back cover design: Jeff Clark
Interior design: Warren C. Jefferson

PETA would like to thank Bryanna Clark Grogan and Louise Hagler for their generous contribution of recipes for this cookbook.

Book Publishing Company
P.O. Box 99
Summertown, TN 38483
1-888-260-8458

Printed in Canada.

06 05 04 03 02 01   6 5 4 3

ISBN 1-57067-044-7

Cooking with PETA : great vegan recipes for a compassionate kitchen / edited by People for the Ethical Treatment of Animals.
      p.   cm.
  Includes index.
  ISBN 1-57067-044-7 (alk. paper)
  1. Vegan cookery. I. People for the Ethical Treatment of Animals.
TX837.C599   1997   97-17909
641.5′636--dc21   CIP

Calculations for the nutritional analyses in this book are based on the average number of servings listed with the recipes and the average amount of an ingredient, if a range is called for. Calculations are rounded up to the nearest gram. If two options for an ingredient are listed, the first one is used. Not included are optional ingredients, serving suggestions, or fat used for frying, unless the amount of fat is specified in the recipe.

CONTENTS

Foreword by Neal D. Barnard, M.D. • 5

Introduction by Ingrid E. Newkirk, President of PETA • 6

Basics • 17

Breakfast • 27

Snacks & Appetizers • 39

Soups • 57

Salads & Salad Dressings • 73

Sandwiches • 95

Main Dishes • 105

Side Dishes • 143

Baked Goods & Spreads • 155

Desserts • 167

Drinks • 199

Glossary of Ingredients • 207

Resources • 212

Index • 217

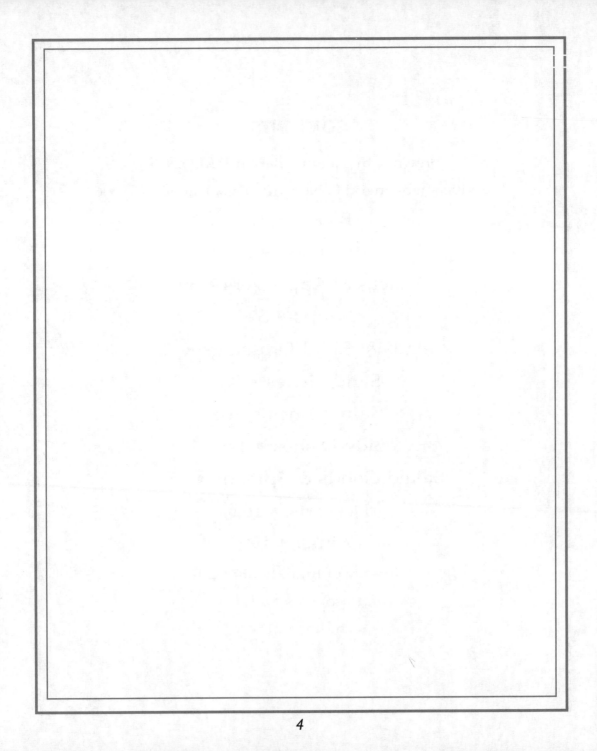

FOREWORD

There is a reason why so many people are going vegetarian these days. Vegetarian foods are terrific for your health. They can boost your energy level, get you into a leaner body, strengthen your immune system, and help you reach a level of health you may not have thought possible. Vegetarian diets are used in programs to actually clean out clogged arteries, reverse heart disease, and help patients with diabetes and high blood pressure get off their medications. Top athletes from Martina Navratilova to Carl Lewis use vegetarian diets to keep themselves in winning form.

But a vegetarian meal does more than that. It helps the Earth breathe more easily. Turning wheat into pasta or beans into hot, hearty soup is so much simpler and more efficient than feeding enormous amounts of grain to cattle or chickens to produce a much smaller amount of meat.

It will let the animals breathe more easily too. The millions of animals on farms (that nowadays are more like factories) would sing your praises with every vegetarian choice you make, if they could.

Revolutionizing your diet is easy. When you think about it, most people have about eight or nine favorite recipes that they tend to choose from. Here are three quick steps to make your favorites vegetarian:

First, think of three meals you like already that happen to be vegetarian. For example, how about spaghetti with tomato sauce, vegetarian chili, or bean burritos?

Second, choose three recipes that you can modify to become vegetarian. For example, split pea soup is just as good without the ham. A taco is great made with beans instead of meat.

Third, try out three new recipes from this book. Have fun as you experiment with delightful new tastes and healthful ingredients. When you've found your three new hits, you've done it! You've now got nine delicious, tasty vegetarian choices.

The Earth will thank you, the animals will thank you, and your body will thank you too.

Neal D. Barnard, M.D.
President, Physicians Committee
for Responsible Medicine

INTRODUCTION

These are exciting times in which to eat! Vegetarianism has become a household word—and practice—and veggie food is one of the hottest things around.

The explosion of vegetarian foods means you can pop everything from bean tacos to veggie "sausage" into the microwave and finish the meal with frozen nondairy "ice cream." You may even be able to order a latte with soymilk in your neighborhood coffee shop and enjoy a veggie burger at the ball game. You can definitely stock your kitchen with wonderful products we could only dream of 20 years ago: flavored rice mixes; microwavable tofu entrées with exotic sauces; soy-based cheeses, mayonnaise, and milk; and imitation meat products that can be used on their own or in your favorite recipes.

Veggie food isn't just a treat for our taste buds; it's great for our health, too. What we eat directly affects the quality of our lives. While animal foods contribute to cancer, heart disease, and many other top killers, fruits, vegetables, beans, and whole grains can actually make us healthy.

With the right food selections, you can lose weight permanently, prevent heart attacks, and even reverse existing heart disease. Studies have shown that vegetarians have stronger immune systems than meat-eaters and that meat-eaters are almost twice as likely to die of heart disease and 60 percent more likely to die of cancer. Meat and dairy consumption also is linked with diabetes, arthritis, osteoporosis, clogged arteries, obesity, asthma, and impotence. One 21-year-long study comparing meat-eaters and vegetarians showed that the greater the meat consumption, the greater the death rate from all causes combined.

A vegetarian diet is also vital if we are to work for a compassionate society. Today's intensive agriculture means that, in the United States alone, more than 8 billion cows, calves, pigs, chickens, turkeys, ducks, and other animals are kept in small overcrowded stalls, cages, or crates, where they're often unable to walk or turn around. Deprived of all things they hold precious, including exercise, sunlight, and even the feel of grass under their feet, these thinking, feeling beings suffer terribly and are slaughtered every day for steaks, burgers, nuggets, patties, and wieners.

It's also important to take things a step further by going vegan—avoiding not only foods containing parts of cows, pigs, turkeys, chickens, and fish, but those containing eggs and dairy, too.

Why avoid these foods? In order to continue producing milk, cows are kept almost constantly pregnant, their babies dragged away within a day or two of birth so humans can drink the milk nature intended for the calves. "Useless" on a dairy farm, the male calves are raised in infamous "veal crates." Females follow in their mothers' hoofprints and are slaughtered when their milk production wanes, usually before their fourth birthday.

Laying hens are among the most pathetic of animals raised on today's factory farms. Squeezed inside tiny, crowded cages, hens live with up to five others on floor space the size of a record album cover. "Spent" chickens are slaughtered for chicken soup and "nuggets."

Fortunately, it's easy to "live and let live," and this book will show you how. From backyard barbecues to elegant dinners, the delicious, healthful, and humane recipes in the following chapters will help you enjoy a long, healthy life, while *you* take care of the animals, the Earth, and your taste buds all at the same time.

Ingrid E. Newkirk, President
People for the Ethical Treatment of Animals

Marvelous Mock Meats

Beans may work for burritos, but how can you re-create your grandmother's recipe for chicken pot pie? Or Mom's marvelous meat loaf? Mock meats to the rescue!

Health food stores and, increasingly, many mainstream supermarkets, carry an amazing array of fab fakes—everything from soy-based hot dogs, burgers, and deli slices to tempeh bacon, chicken-flavored wheat meat, and ground beef and sausage substitutes. If you're new to vegetarianism, you may think that last sentence was in a foreign language. Tempeh? Wheat meat? These, along with tofu and textured vegetable protein, are excellent plant-based sources of protein that will satisfy any "meat tooth."

Seitan (or "wheat meat") is a hearty meat alternative made of wheat gluten. Seitan is very versatile and can be grilled, sautéed, or shaped and stuffed for vegetarian roasts. Most health food stores carry ready-made seitan products; instant gluten flour mixes, used to make wheat meat, are also available.

Tempeh, made from fermented soybeans, is another hearty meat substitute. It can be sliced for sandwiches, cubed for kebabs, or grated and used in place of ground meat. Before adding tempeh to recipes, steam it for 15 minutes to stop the fermenting process.

Tofu, also known as bean curd, is a protein-rich food made from soybeans. It comes in a variety of textures and can be used to replace not only meat, but also eggs and dairy products.

Textured vegetable protein (TVP) is made from low-fat soy flour which has been processed into chunks of various sizes. It has the fooled-you mouth-feel of meat. Try it in your favorite loaf recipe or in chili and sloppy joes.

Can You Do Tofu?

Even the most courageous cook can turn cowardly when it comes to tofu. But this culinary chameleon easily absorbs the flavors of other ingredients, and that's what makes it so versatile. Tofu's many textures also increase its adaptability. Soft tofu can be blended to make creamy dressings, dips, puddings, and pie fillings. Firm tofu will hold its shape when sliced and diced—perfect for stir-frying or baking. Tofu can also be drained or frozen to change its texture even more.

- *Draining*: To make tofu firmer, drain it in a colander. Simply place the colander over a bowl, and leave it on the counter for up to 30 minutes or in the fridge.

- *Pressing*: Pressing the water out of tofu allows it to absorb more flavors during cooking. When draining tofu, cover it with a weight, such as a bowl filled with dried beans. For a power press, wrap the tofu in a clean towel, and place it between two baking sheets. Put a heavy weight on top, and pop the whole thing in the fridge for an hour or more.

- *Freezing*: Freezing tofu makes it chewy—ideal for chili or mock tuna salad. Drain the tofu, place it in a plastic bag, and freeze for at least 24 hours (up to several months). The tofu will turn a yellowish-tan color—don't panic! Before using frozen tofu, thaw it in the refrigerator, then squeeze out the excess moisture.

Dairy-Free and Delicious

Mock meat isn't the only "faux fare" you'll find in natural food stores. Dairy-free alternatives include calcium-fortified soymilks; soy-based cream cheese, yogurt, and sour cream; nondairy frozen desserts; and even chocolate made with tofu instead of milk.

In baked goods, cow's milk can be replaced with an equal amount of soymilk or other nondairy alternative, such as rice or oat milk. Instead of buttermilk, stir 2 teaspoons lemon juice into 1 cup of soymilk. Replace sour milk or plain yogurt when baking by mixing 1 teaspoon apple cider vinegar with 1 cup of soymilk.

Eggs-citing Eggless Eggs

One egg (or even two) in a recipe can often simply be skipped, but there are also many tried and true substitutes that work wonders.

Crumbled and seasoned tofu makes delicious morning scrambles and eggless salad. And look for eggless mayonnaise, scrambled tofu mixes, and other egg alternatives in your local health food store.

Binding for burgers and loaves:
- Mashed potato or avocado
- Moistened bread crumbs or rolled oats
- Tahini (sesame butter) and nut butters
- Whole wheat flour

Baking (each substitute replaces one egg):
- Commercial egg replacer (for example, 1½ teaspoons ENER-G + 2 tablespoons water)
- 3 tablespoons tofu blended with the liquid in the recipe
- 2 tablespoons cornstarch, potato starch, or arrowroot mixed with 2 tablespoons water
- 1 heaping tablespoon soy flour + 2 tablespoons water
- ½ banana, mashed
- 1 tablespoon flax seeds + ½ cup water whipped in a blender or beaten with egg beaters for 1 to 2 minutes, or until the mixture is thick and has the consistency of beaten egg whites

Veggie Kids

The list of adult illnesses stemming from a meat- and dairy-based diet reads like a Who's Who of modern-day killers—heart disease, cancer, high blood pressure, stroke. But what about kids—don't they need meat and milk to stay healthy? No way! Cow's milk has been linked to asthma, allergies, anemia, and intestinal bleeding, and meat is loaded with artery-clogging fat! Besides, plenty of plant foods—including broccoli, tofu, dried figs, and fortified orange juice—contain calcium. Raisins, almonds, beans, and blackstrap molasses (a great sweetener for kids' morning oatmeal) are good sources of iron. And nut butters, beans, and whole grains are packed with protein.

But what if the only "vegetables" your kids will eat are french fries and ketchup? Try these tried-and-true tips:

• Grab an apron and put your kids to work! Kids are much more likely to eat meals they've helped prepare. Even pint-sized chefs can do basic tasks such as washing fruit and stirring together ingredients. Let children help plan weekly menus, and take tots on "field trips" to farmers' markets to pick out fresh fruits and veggies.

• Your mama might not approve, but encourage kids to play with their food. Spread peanut butter on bagel halves, and let kids make funny faces or designs with colorful diced fruits and nuts. Or, using a cookie cutter, cut whole wheat bread into dinosaur shapes for silly sandwiches.

• Designate "kids only" sections in your refrigerator and pantry where ready-to-eat snacks are always available. Kids will be less likely to grab greasy chips if more healthful foods—like veggie sticks with mild salsa for dipping, or mini fruit-and-nut muffins—are on hand.

• If your kids don't take to healthful fare at first, play a game of vegetable hide-and-eat. Sneak diced and grated veggies into everything from corn muffins to tomato soup. Dried and fresh fruits can be tucked into cookies, quick breads, or pancakes (fruit can do double-duty if you top pancakes with puréed berries instead of maple syrup).

Need more ideas?

These easy recipes have been kid-tested and approved:

Golden Vegetable Noodle Soup, p. 59
Tasty "Toona" Salad, p. 87
Chick-Pea Pita Pockets, p. 96
Nouveau Sloppy Joes, p. 101
Un-Chicken Filet, p. 104
Chicken-Friendly Tofu Nuggets
With Maple-Mustard Dipping Sauce, p. 110
Crispy Tofu Cubes, p. 113
Funny-Face Burritos, p. 118
Cocoa-Banana Muffins, p. 159
Nuttin' Butter Spread, p. 165
Crispy Rice Treats, p. 184
Chocolate Pudding, p. 191
Carob-Peanut Butter Smoothie, p. 200

Vegetarianism is not just good for animals, it's good for you too.

Breakfast of Champions?

It's hard to imagine a more unhealthful way to start the day than the typical American breakfast. Every time you eat a typical bacon-and-egg breakfast, you swallow a whopping dose of artery-clogging saturated fat and cholesterol. Egg yolks each contain a whopping 213 mg of cholesterol; serving up just one of these cholesterol bombs for breakfast every morning can raise your cholesterol level by as much as 10 points! In fact, women who eat eggs daily triple their risk of breast cancer. And the higher your cholesterol, the more likely you are to develop coronary artery disease—the top killer of Americans.

The good news is that cholesterol levels often drop 25 percent or more with a switch to a vegan diet—and that lowers your risk of heart disease by 50 percent or more!

What's the Skinny on Beef?

For starters, the number-one killer of Americans is heart disease, caused largely by cholesterol- and fat-laden meat. Even "extra-lean" ground beef is about 54 percent fat. And there's more: Beef is the most common culprit in cases of E. coli poisoning, which 20,000 Americans suffer from every year, with up to 500 of them dying from it.

Wait, Don't Throw That Burger on the Grill!

If reports of tainted fast-food burgers aren't enough to make you vow to give beef the boot, food safety experts say the greatest risk of illness is posed by flesh cooked on backyard barbecue grills. According to the Centers for Disease Control and Prevention, about 6.5 million people become ill and 9,100 die each year from acute food poisoning, many from undercooked barbecued burgers.

In addition, certain preparation methods such as smoking or charring increase cancer risks, according to the American Cancer Society. Hamburger smoke curling off the grill contains 27 different dangerous compounds, including hydrocarbons, furans, steroids, and pesticide residues.

Want to Eat Healthfully? Then Get the Chicken Out of Your Kitchen!

Even if you don't eat the skin, throw away the dark meat, and use a nonfat cooking method, chicken still contains 23 percent fat—much more than most grains, vegetables, fruits, and beans. It also contains as much cholesterol as beef. To make matters worse, up to 90 percent of federally inspected poultry is infected with bacteria like salmonella and campylobacter.

Think Turkey Is a Nutritious Food? Think Again.

Some cuts of turkey can be almost as high in fat and cholesterol as lean ground beef. A roasted turkey's leg contains 72 milligrams of cholesterol and is 47 percent fat. Ground turkey products derive as much as 59 percent of their calories from fat.

Turkey, like other meats, is a breeding ground for bacteria. An estimated 2 million people in the U.S. become ill each year from salmonella. This dangerous type of bacteria has survived as long as 13 months on the skin of frozen turkeys.

And let's not forget the chemical cocktails turkeys are injected with to fight disease and enhance growth. Two of these substances, Ipronidazole and dimetridazole, are carcinogenic to humans.

Fact or Fish Story: Is "Seafood" Really Good for You?

Have you eliminated meat from your diet but drawn the line at fish because it's "healthful"? On the surface, eating "seafood" seems like the answer to cutting saturated fats, cholesterol, and calories and combatting heart disease. But eating seafood does have a catch.

According to the Centers for Disease Control, seafood is the single largest source of food-borne illness. Raw shellfish is the absolute riskiest food you can put into your mouth, but other kinds of fish are close runners-up.

In addition to being contaminated with bacteria, many fish are contaminated with natural toxins, such as ciguatera and scromboid, as well as environmental toxins like PCBs, mercury, DDT, and dioxin.

Due to widespread water pollution, seafood is the largest dietary source of toxic chemicals and pesticides, which can cause cancer. Top-of-the-line predators like salmon and trout can absorb so many toxins from eating contaminated smaller fish that they themselves are unsafe to eat. Halibut, tuna, and swordfish, may accumulate enough methylmercury to cause nerve damage. Shellfish can accumulate large amounts of contaminants simply because so much of it passes through their bodies as they feed.

The main reason people eat fish is to obtain omega-3 fatty acids (believed to help prevent heart disease). But omega-3s can be readily found in many vegetarian foods, including flaxseed oil, evening primrose oil, canola and olive oils, walnuts, alfalfa sprouts, spinach, and soybeans.

Milk Is a Natural—for Calves

Cow's milk is meant for baby calves, who have four stomachs, double their weight in 47 days, and are destined to weigh 300 pounds within a year. In humans, milk has been linked to heart disease, some cancers, diabetes, and even osteoporosis, the very disease the dairy industry claims it prevents! (The high animal protein content of milk actually causes calcium to be leached from the body.)

Milk is also loaded with fat and cholesterol and contains an ever-increasing variety of pesticides and antibiotics fed to cows.

The good news is that you can get all the calcium you need from the plant world: Tofu, broccoli, kale, dried fruits, nuts, seeds, beans and other legumes, grains, and calcium-fortified orange juice are all good sources.

Pork: The "Other" White Meat?

The pork industry is desperately trying to boost sales by calling pork "the other white meat," thereby trying to suggest that pork is low in fat and cholesterol. But even true white meats are not health foods. They contain substantial amounts of cholesterol, fat, and bacteria, leaving out fiber, complex carbohydrates, and vitamin C.

But back to pork: A pork shoulder cut, even with the fat cut off, still gets 55 percent of its calories from fat and packs more than 100 mg of cholesterol in just a 4-ounce serving. Over the long run, pork, like other animal products, can drive cholesterol levels up, increase cancer risk, and contribute to obesity.

Pork is often contaminated with trichina worms, salmonella, staphylococci, and clostridia. Thorough cooking will kill these microorganisms, but it will not kill those deposited on carving knives, cutting boards, or kitchen sponges when the raw meat is unwrapped and cut.

Because chemicals become concentrated in animal flesh, pork is also a source of unwanted residues, including pesticides, antibiotics, sulfa drugs, and halocarbons.

The fact is that meat, by any other name, is not a nutritious food.

BASICS

copyright Peter Max 1997

"As long as human beings will go on shedding the blood of animals, there will never be any peace."

—Isaac Bashevis Singer

MARINARA MADNESS

This fat-free basic Italian sauce can be varied endlessly by adding herbs and vegetables. Serve as is for a chunky topping, or blend when cooled for a smooth sauce.

Yield: about 4½ cups

½ cup water
1 medium onion, chopped
1 small green pepper, chopped
2 cloves garlic, crushed
1 small carrot, chopped
¼ cup chopped fresh parsley
1 (28-oz.) can crushed tomatoes
½ cup chopped fresh basil,
   or 2 tablespoons dried basil
2 tablespoons chopped fresh
   oregano, or 2 teaspoons dried
   oregano
1 teaspoon salt
¼ teaspoon freshly ground black
   pepper

Simmer the onion, green pepper, garlic, carrot, and parsley together in the water until almost tender.

Add the tomatoes, basil, oregano, salt, and pepper, and simmer for about 20 minutes. Cool and blend until smooth in a food processor or blender.

Per ½ cup: Calories 30, Protein 1 g, Fat 0 g, Carbohydrates 6 g,
Calcium 26 mg, Fiber 2 g, Sodium 250 mg

MELTY PIZZA "CHEESE"

This easy recipe is tastier than any commercial vegan cheese substitute and much cheaper. It also makes great grilled "cheese" sandwiches. The nutritional yeast adds protein and lots of B-complex vitamins.

Yield: 1 ¼ cups

Place all the ingredients, except the water and optional oil, in a blender, and blend until smooth. Pour the mixture into a small saucepan, and stir over medium heat until it starts to thicken, then let it bubble for 30 seconds. Whisk vigorously.

Microwave Option: Pour the mixture into a microwave-proof bowl; cover and cook on HIGH for 2 minutes. Whisk, then microwave for 2 more minutes, and whisk again.

Whisk in the water and optional oil. The oil adds richness and helps it melt better, but the "cheese" still only contains 2.6 g of fat per ¼ cup.

Drizzle immediately over pizza or other food, and broil or bake until a skin forms on top. Alternatively, refrigerate in a small, covered plastic container for up to a week. It will become quite firm when chilled but will still remain spreadable. You can spread the firm "cheese" on bread or quesadillas for grilling, or heat it to spread more thinly on casseroles, etc.

1 cup water
¼ cup nutritional yeast
2 tablespoons cornstarch
1 tablespoon flour
1 teaspoon lemon juice
½ teaspoon salt
¼ teaspoon garlic granules
4 teaspoons calcium carbonate powder (optional)*
2 tablespoons water
1 tablespoon canola oil (optional)

*(The optional added calcium carbonate powder gives 2 tablespoons of the "cheese" about the same amount of calcium as 1 oz. of dairy cheese.)

Per ¼ cup: Calories 37, Protein 3 g, Fat 0 g, Carbohydrates 6 g, Calcium 18 mg, Fiber 0 g, Sodium 221 mg

BASICS

SOY-FREE CREAM CHEESE

If you're allergic to soy or just want a change of pace, try this tasty version of everyone's favorite spread.

1 cup unflavored nondairy milk
2¾ tablespoons quick oats
3 tablespoons raw cashew butter
   (or ¼ cup raw cashews, finely
   ground in a coffee/spice grinder)
½-1 tablespoon cornstarch
   (depending upon how soft you
   want it)
1 teaspoon lemon juice
⅛-¼ teaspoon salt

In a blender, mix ½ cup of the milk and the oatmeal until the mixture is fairly smooth. Add the rest of the ingredients. Blend until VERY smooth. Pour the mixture into a small saucepan, and whisk constantly over medium-high heat until thick and smooth.

Microwave Option: Microwave the mixture in a medium-sized microwave-safe bowl or glass measuring beaker, covered with a plate, on HIGH for 1½ minutes. Whisk well, then cook on HIGH for another 2 minutes. Whisk again.

Scrape the mixture into a hard plastic container with a lid, and refrigerate.

Per 2 tablespoons: Calories 38, Protein 1 g, Fat 1 g, Carbohydrates 5 g, Calcium 4 mg, Fiber 0 g, Sodium 47 mg

TOFU CREAM CHEESE SPREAD

Cashew butter mixed with silken tofu gives you a miracle product: the taste and texture of traditional cream cheese with none of the cholesterol and half the fat. You can use low-fat silken tofu in this recipe and still get delicious results.

Yield: 1 cup

Place the tofu in a clean tea towel, gather the end up, and twist and squeeze for a couple of minutes to extract most of the water. Crumble into the processing bowl of a food processor with the remaining ingredients, and process for several minutes until the mixture is VERY smooth. (You may have to stop the machine and loosen the mixture with a spatula once or twice.) Use right away or scrape into a covered container and refrigerate. It firms up with refrigeration.

1 (12.3 oz.) pkg. extra-firm silken tofu (1½ cups), squeezed in a towel
3½ tablespoons cashew butter, or 5 tablespoons raw cashews, finely ground
4½ teaspoons lemon juice
½ teaspoon salt
1 teaspoon liquid sweetener (optional)

B A S I C S

Per 2 tablespoons: Calories 61, Protein 4 g, Fat 5 g, Carbohydrates 3 g, Calcium 16 mg, Fiber 1 g, Sodium 149 mg.

FRANKLY FAKE FETA

Try this "feta" in salads and sandwiches, or just to nibble on by itself. You can also use low-fat tofu in this recipe and still get delicious results.

Yield: 2 cups

1 lb. extra-firm regular or silken tofu
1 cup water
½ cup light miso
2 tablespoons lemon juice or white wine vinegar
1 teaspoon salt

Cut the tofu into slices or cubes. Combine the remaining ingredients to make a marinade, and pour over the tofu.

Keep this refrigerated in a covered jar for up to three weeks, shaking the jar every day. Use in salads.

Per ½ cup: Calories 159, Protein 11 g, Fat 7 g, Carbohydrates 12 g, Calcium 146 mg, Fiber 2 g, Sodium 541 mg

Going vegetarian could save your life! The average American man has a 50 percent chance of dying of a heart attack, but vegetarian men have only a 4 percent risk.

TOFU MAYONNAISE

Silken tofu makes a smooth, thick, rich-tasting mayonnaise that doesn't separate easily and needs no oil. You can use low-fat tofu in this recipe and still get delicious results.

Yield: 1¾ cups

Combine all the ingredients in a blender until very smooth. This will keep about 2 weeks in the refrigerator.

Use this recipe as a base for the flavored mayonnaise variations below.

Aioli: To make a garlic dip for cold, steamed vegetables and artichokes, use lemon juice, omit the mustard, and add 4 cloves peeled garlic while blending. This is also a good spread for making garlic toast.

Tofu "Hollandaise": Use lemon juice instead of vinegar, and omit the mustard. Use soft silken tofu and heat gently just before serving. Add herbs such as dill, tarragon, or basil to taste. For a tangier sauce, add ½ teaspoon cumin and a pinch of cayenne.

Tofu Tartar Sauce: Add ½ cup chopped onion and ½ cup chopped dill pickle, with some of the pickle brine to taste. If you have no pickles, use chopped cucumber with dillweed and white wine vinegar to taste.

Easy Cole Slaw Dressing: Mix the basic Tofu Mayonnaise with any kind of fruit juice until it is thin enough and sweet enough for your taste.

1 (12.3 oz.) pkg. extra-firm or firm silken tofu (1½ cups)
2 tablespoons apple cider vinegar or lemon juice
1⅛ teaspoons salt
½ teaspoon dry mustard
⅛ teaspoon white pepper
1 teaspoon sweetener of your choice (optional)

Per 2 tablespoons: Calories 16, Protein 2 g, Fat 1 g, Carbohydrates 1 g, Calcium 8 mg, Fiber 0 g, Sodium 180 mg

BASICS

SWEET CREAM TOPPING

Warning: This take on whipped cream might steal the show from the dessert it tops!

Yield: 1 ½ cups

½ lb. firm tofu
¼ cup oil
¼ cup confectioner's sugar
1 teaspoon vanilla
½ teaspoon lemon juice
⅛ teaspoon salt

Combine all the ingredients in a blender, and blend until smooth and creamy. Chill and serve as you would whipped cream.

Per ¼ cup: Calories 129, Protein 3 g, Fat 10 g, Carbohydrates 7 g, Calcium 40 mg, Fiber 0 g, Sodium 49 mg

TOFU SOUR CREAM

A versatile staple item that's simple to make.

Yield: about 1 cup

½ lb. firm tofu
2 tablespoons oil
1 tablespoon fresh lemon juice
1½ teaspoons sweetener of your choice
½ teaspoon salt

Combine all the ingredients in a blender, and blend until smooth and creamy. This will keep in your refrigerator for 5 to 7 days.

Per tablespoon: Calories 28, Protein 1 g, Fat 2 g, Carbohydrates 1 g, Calcium 15 mg, Fiber 1 g, Sodium 68 mg

VEGGIE WORCESTERSHIRE SAUCE

The classic taste of Worcestershire, minus the anchovies.

Yield: 1 ½ cups

Combine all the ingredients in a blender. Pour into a saucepan and bring to a boil. Store in the refrigerator.

1 cup cider vinegar
⅓ cup dark molasses
¼ cup soy sauce or mushroom soy sauce
¼ cup water
3 tablespoons lemon juice
1½ teaspoons salt
1½ teaspoons mustard powder
1 teaspoon onion powder
¾ teaspoon ground ginger
½ teaspoon black pepper
¼ teaspoon garlic granules
¼ teaspoon cayenne pepper
¼ teaspoon ground cinnamon
⅛ teaspoon ground cloves or allspice
⅛ teaspoon ground cardamom

Per tablespoon: Calories 20, Protein 0 g, Fat 0 g, Carbohydrates 5 g, Calcium 7 mg, Fiber 0 g, Sodium 307 mg

BUTTERSCOTCH

It was the cutest thing I ever saw and the most amazing. I had just parked my car and was walking down the long path to Georgi and Don Small's rambling white house, when this little tan and gold hen came running to meet me. When she was right in front of me, she looked up at me and began bouncing up and down. My mouth dropped open at the sight. Then I realized she was jumping; she only appeared to be bouncing because each tiny swift hop only took her two or three inches into the air. But what she lacked in power, she made up for in determination. The bouncing continued as Georgi came up behind her.

"Butterscotch wants you to pick her up," she said, laughing. She lifted her up and put her into my arms, a thick, soft mass of feathers with a small warm body inside. The little hen nestled right in, as content and cuddly as any creature I've ever held, and gazed up at me as if to say, "Isn't this nice?"

Georgi said that after Butterscotch hatched, her mother abandoned her. So Georgi raised her in the house for the first few months of her life. Then gradually, she weaned her back to the outside, where she has freedom, a barn with plenty of straw-filled nooks, and many companion chickens—none in any danger because the Smalls are vegetarians.

When I house-sat for Don and Georgi, I got to know Butterscotch well. She was adorable. Each time I went out to feed the sheep, horse, ducks, and others, she appeared immediately and led the way. She had the routine down pat. What a friendly companion she was, as devoted as a family dog, but in her own charming way.

—Carla Bennett

BREAKFAST & BREADS

copyright Peter Max 1997

"I'm living proof you don't need animal flesh to be strong. Some of the world's greatest athletes are vegetarians."

—Martina Navratilova

BREAKFAST CASSEROLE

An ideal one-dish meal for big family breakfasts. Serve it to visiting friends and relatives, and they'll be clamoring for the recipe!

Yield: 8 servings

3 cups cooked potatoes, mashed,
  but not peeled
1½ lbs. firm tofu, mashed
2 tablespoons soy sauce
1 medium onion, chopped
2 cloves garlic, crushed
2 tablespoons olive oil
2 tablespoons parsley
2 teaspoons basil
½ teaspoon black pepper
Paprika

Mix together the potatoes, tofu, and soy sauce. Sauté the onion and garlic in the oil until translucent. Preheat the oven to 325°F. Mix the onion and garlic into the potato mixture, and add the parsley, basil, and black pepper. Spread into an oiled 8 x 8 x 2-inch baking dish. Sprinkle with paprika and bake for 35 minutes.

Per serving: Calories 157, Protein 7 g, Fat 6 g, Carbohydrates 16 g,
Calcium 103 mg, Fiber 2 g, Sodium 262 mg

SOUTHWEST SCRAMBLES

Tofu makes egg-free omelettes, quiches, and scrambles easy! Try a variety of seasonings and fresh vegetables (such as broccoli, carrots, black olives, etc.) when making this dish until you find the combination you enjoy most.

Sauté the onion and garlic in the oil until the onion is soft. Add the mushrooms, cover, and continue to sauté until the mushrooms are soft. Add the green or yellow pepper and the chili pepper, and cook for a few more minutes. Add the tofu, salt, and curry powder, and mix well. Continue to cook until the tofu is heated. Serve with salsa on top with toast on the side or in a heated flour tortilla.

1 medium onion, chopped
2 cloves garlic, crushed
2 tablespoons oil
4 oz. mushrooms, sliced
1 green or yellow bell pepper, diced
1 chili pepper, seeded and diced
1 lb. firm or extra firm tofu, patted dry and crumbled
½ teaspoon salt
1 teaspoon curry powder
Salsa

Per serving: Calories 357, Protein 18 g, Fat 22 g, Carbohydrates 17 g, Calcium 276 mg, Fiber 4 g, Sodium 557 mg

SCRAMBLE-ICIOUS IDEAS

The possibilities for scrambled tofu are limited only by your imagination. Wrap Tex-Mex Scrambles in a tortilla to make a "breakfast burrito" (add refried beans, home fries, and/or salsa for variety). Grated cheddar-style soy cheese adds a rich, zesty flavor. Or try Italian scrambles with oregano, diced tomatoes, and Parmesan-flavored soy "cheese." Go Greek with chopped spinach and hummus (added at the last minute). Or try tossing in standard breakfast fare like soy sausage and diced potatoes. For the less adventurous, try basic scrambles with a teaspoon of onion powder, a dash of turmeric (for color), and salt to taste.

BREAKFAST

SIMPLY SUPERB CRÊPES

Enjoy these crêpes by themselves or as a base for sweet fillings and sauces. Try them spread with jelly or applesauce or filled with Southwest Scrambles (p. 29). You can even use them in place of noodles for manicotti.

Yield: 9 (10-inch) crêpes

½ cup unbleached white flour
½ cup whole wheat pastry flour
¼ cup soy flour
¼ cup nutritional yeast (optional)
½ teaspoon baking powder
½ teaspoon salt
3 cups soymilk

Mix the dry ingredients and make a well in the middle. Pour in the soymilk and whip together. The batter should be very thin.

Heat a 10-inch nonstick crêpe pan over moderate heat, and spray with non-stick spray. Pour in about ⅓ cup of the batter, tilting and moving the pan so that the batter covers the bottom of the pan with a thin coating. Cook until it is browned underneath and starts to pull away from the edge of the pan. Carefully flip it over and brown on the other side. Serve hot.

Per crêpe: Calories 85, Protein 5 g, Fat 2 g, Carbohydrates 12 g, Calcium 35 mg, Fiber 2 g, Sodium 152 mg

TEMPTING TEMPEH STICKS

These sticks can be served as a side dish to pancakes, waffles, or French toast or by themselves as finger food.

Yield: 12 to 16 sticks

Steam the tempeh for 20 minutes, and cut into ¼ to ½-inch sticks. Mix together the water, soy sauce, garlic, and chipotle. Fry the tempeh sticks in 1 tablespoon olive oil over medium heat until browned. Add ½ tablespoon olive oil, and brown on the other side. Pour the liquid evenly over the sticks, and simmer until it is evaporated. Serve hot or cold.

½ lb. tempeh
3 tablespoons water
1½ tablespoons soy sauce
1 clove garlic, pressed
⅛ teaspoon chipotle chili powder
    (optional)
1½ tablespoons olive oil

Per 2 sticks: Calories 93, Protein 7 g, Fat 5 g, Carbohydrates 6 g,
Calcium 32 mg, Fiber 2 g, Sodium 217 mg

BETTER THAN BACON

It's bacon with a makeover—no oil, no cholesterol, no meat! To make it extra crunchy, dry it in an electric home food dehydrator. You can use low-fat tofu in this recipe and still get delicious results.

Yield: about 40 thin slices

½ cup soy sauce (low-sodium, if available)
1 tablespoon nutritional yeast flakes
1 tablespoon maple syrup
½ tablespoon liquid smoke
½ lb. extra-firm regular tofu

Mix the soy sauce, yeast flakes, maple syrup, and liquid smoke together in a shallow container. With a cheese slicer, shave the tofu into very thin slices. Marinate the tofu in the soy sauce mixture for 1 day or more.

To cook, heat a lightly oiled, heavy skillet or nonstick griddle over medium high heat. When the pan is hot, fry the tofu slices until they are golden-brown and almost crispy on both sides, scraping underneath the slices as you turn them with a sturdy spatula. Turn several times during cooking, and cool in the pan (it crisps up as it cools).

This makes excellent "BLT" sandwiches and can be crumbled or diced and added to other dishes for a bacon-like flavor.

Per slice: Calories 9, Protein 1 g, Fat 0 g, Carbohydrates 1 g, Calcium 7 mg, Fiber 0 g, Sodium 121 mg

MOCK SAUSAGE

These patties can be refrigerated or frozen and reheated in an oven or skillet or on a grill. The cooked mixture can be crumbled into other dishes. You can also use low-fat tofu and still get delicious results.

Yield: 10 patties or 20 links

In a bowl, pour the water and soy sauce over the textured vegetable protein. When soft, add all the other ingredients, except the gluten flour, and mix well.

When the mixture is cool, add the gluten flour. Mix well with your hands, then shape into 10 thin patties or 20 small "sausage links." Steam-fry in two batches in a lightly oiled heavy skillet over medium heat, covered, until firm and browned (7 to 10 minutes per side for patties; at least 20 minutes total for links). These can be refrigerated or frozen for later use. To reheat, place in a covered, lightly oiled skillet with a few tablespoons of water, and cook over high heat until the water has evaporated.

Mock Italian Sausage: Make as for Mock Sausage, increasing the onion powder to 1 teaspoon. Omit the sage and marjoram. Add ¾ teaspoon ground fennel or anise, 2 tablespoons balsamic or red wine vinegar (or dry red wine), 1 teaspoon dried oregano (or 1 tablespoon fresh), and 1 teaspoon basil (or 1 tablespoon fresh). Use ½-1 teaspoon red pepper flakes.

¾ cup boiling water
2 tablespoons soy sauce
1 cup dry textured vegetable protein granules
½ cup mashed firm or medium-firm tofu
2 teaspoons crumbled sage leaves
1 teaspoon marjoram
½ teaspoon garlic granules
½ teaspoon onion powder
½ teaspoon thyme
½ teaspoon salt
½ teaspoon red pepper flakes
Black pepper, to taste
1 teaspoon liquid smoke (optional)
½ cup instant gluten flour (vital wheat gluten), or unbleached flour

Per patty: Calories 66, Protein 11 g, Fat 0 g, Carbohydrates 4 g, Calcium 34 mg, Fiber 1 g, Sodium 204 mg

WAKE-'EM-UP PANCAKES

Not a morning person? These pancakes, with their fruity twist, will put a smile on your face! You can also use low-fat soy products in this recipe and still get delicious results.

Yield: about 24 (4-inch) pancakes

2½ cups whole wheat pastry flour, unbleached white flour, or a combination
¼ cup soymilk powder or soy flour (optional)
4 teaspoons baking powder
2 teaspoons baking soda
1 teaspoon salt
3 cups fruit juice (apple, orange, etc.)

In a large bowl, mix together the dry ingredients. When they are well-combined, stir in the fruit juice. Mix briefly—lumps are okay.

Heat a nonstick griddle or skillet (or a lightly oiled heavy skillet) over high heat until hot, then turn it down to medium high. Spoon the batter onto the pan, making 4-inch (silver dollar) pancakes. When the tops are bubbly, turn them over carefully and cook until the underside is golden and the middle is cooked. You can spread apart one pancake using a fork to test. Serve immediately with maple syrup or other toppings.

Per pancake: Calories 57, Protein 2 g, Fat 0 g, Carbohydrates 12 g, Calcium 15 mg, Fiber 1 g, Sodium 90 mg

FRENCH TOAST ROYALE

You won't miss the butter and eggs usually associated with this breakfast favorite—it's delicious!

Yield: 6 slices of toast

Blend or whisk together all the ingredients (except the bread slices) in a shallow bowl.

Dip the bread slices into this mixture, and cook, either on a nonstick griddle until browned on both sides or on a greased cookie sheet in a 400°F oven until golden on both sides, turning once. For an interesting change of pace, bake the French toast in a nonstick waffle iron until golden-brown.

Serve with maple syrup or your favorite topping.

Banana French Toast: Omit ½ cup soymilk and the flour, and blend the remaining ingredients with 1 ripe banana.

TOP TIP: You can also use low-fat tofu in this recipe and still get delicious results.

1 cup soymilk
2 tablespoons flour
1 tablespoon nutritional yeast flakes
1 teaspoon sugar or sweetener of your choice
1 teaspoon vanilla
½ teaspoon salt
Pinch of nutmeg
6 slices whole wheat bread

Per slice: Calories 80, Protein 4 g, Fat 1 g, Carbohydrates 13 g, Calcium 10 mg, Fiber 3 g, Sodium 284 mg

ERICA'S WONDERFUL WAFFLES

The hint of cinnamon and apples makes these waffles a crowd-pleaser. Top with fresh fruit or jam.

½ cup white flour
½ cup whole wheat flour
2 tablespoons baking powder
1 teaspoon baking soda
½ teaspoon cinnamon
¼ teaspoon salt (optional)
1 cup soymilk
½ cup applesauce

Combine the dry ingredients and mix. Add the soymilk and applesauce, pour into an oiled waffle iron, and cook until golden brown.

TOP TIP: You can turn these into pancakes by adding more liquid.

Per waffle: Calories 266, Protein 10 g, Fat 3 g, Carbohydrates 50 g, Calcium 62 mg, Fiber 7 g, Sodium 19 mg

B
R
E
A
K
F
A
S
T

HOMESTYLE HASH BROWNS

With this breakfast treat waiting in the kitchen, you'll never sleep in again!

Yield: 2 to 3 servings

Sauté the onion and the garlic in the oil until the onions are soft. Add the potatoes to the onion and garlic, and cook until tender. Add salt and pepper to taste.

1 medium onion, finely chopped
1 clove garlic, crushed
2 tablespoons oil
2 large potatoes, grated
Salt and pepper, to taste

Per serving: Calories 257, Protein 2 g, Fat 10 g, Carbohydrates 37 g, Calcium 28 mg, Fiber 4 g, Sodium 10 mg

Twenty thousand pounds of potatoes can be grown on one acre of land, but only 165 pounds of beef can be produced in the same space.

CREAMY COUNTRY GRAVY

This thick, creamy gravy is great with biscuits and potatoes. Use only unflavored soymilk.

½ cup unbleached white flour
2-4 tablespoons nutritional yeast
2 tablespoons canola or soybean oil
4 cups soymilk, or 2 cups soymilk
   and 2 cups water or stock
1 tablespoon soy sauce
3 teaspoons poultry seasoning
2 teaspoons onion powder
½ teaspoon garlic powder
¼ teaspoon freshly ground black
   pepper

Stovetop Method: Toast the flour and nutritional yeast in the oil until it starts to brown. Whip in the soymilk gradually, leaving no lumps. Whip in the soy sauce, poultry seasoning, onion powder, garlic powder, and black pepper. Heat until it thickens and just starts to boil.

Microwave Method: In a 2-quart glass measuring cup, whip together all the ingredients (leaving out the oil if you like). Microwave on HIGH for 4 minutes. Whip until smooth and microwave on HIGH for 4 more minutes. Whip and serve.

Per ½ cup: Calories 94, Protein 5 g, Fat 5 g, Carbohydrates 8 g, Calcium 22 mg, Fiber 2 g, Sodium 128 mg

B R E A K F A S T

SNACKS & APPETIZERS

copyright Peter Max 1997

"I brainwashed youngsters into doing wrong. I want to say sorry to children everywhere for selling out to concerns who make millions by murdering animals."

—Former Ronald McDonald, Geoff Guiliano

APPETIZER TIPS

Appetizers can be as simple as chips and dip or as elegant as a vegetarian pâté. Here are some ideas for quick and easy hors d'oeuvres that will get you out of the kitchen in time to enjoy the party. Whip up a seven-layer Mexican dip using refried beans, black olives, salsa, tortilla chips, tofu sour cream, sliced green onions, and jalapeños. Veganize that old standby, pigs in a blanket, by rolling out a package of puff pastry dough ¼-inch thick. Cut into rectangles and spread each one with Dijon mustard. Wrap the rectangles around tofu hot dogs, and bake in 425°F oven for 10 minutes, then cut each into several pieces.

Marinate bite-sized pieces of tempeh or tofu in your favorite sauce—try barbecue, sweet and sour, or spicy peanut—and chill for several hours. Place in a shallow baking pan, cover with the sauce, and bake at 350°F for several minutes. Spear each piece with a party pick to serve. Always a hit!

Combine your favorite spiced nuts with raisins, dried apricots, pretzels, sunflower seeds, and pumpkin seeds for a marvelous munchie.

BUTTERBEAN, BUTTERBEAN PÂTÉ

This party pâté is bursting with so much flavor, we had to name it twice!

Yield: 10 servings

Heat the oil in a large skillet over medium-high heat. Sauté the garlic, onion, carrot, mushrooms, and parsley until the onion is soft, but not browned (about 5 minutes).

Place the beans, nutritional yeast, and soy sauce in a food processor, and purée until the mixture is smooth. Stir in the sautéed vegetables.

Transfer the pâté to a decorative serving dish, and refrigerate for 1 hour.

TOP TIP: For a smoother pâté, add the sautéed vegetables to the bean mixture while in the food processor, and blend.

1 teaspoon olive oil
2 cloves garlic, minced
1 cup minced onion
⅓ cup minced carrot
⅓ cup minced mushrooms
⅓ cup minced fresh parsley
1½ cups cooked butterbeans
1 tablespoon nutritional yeast
1 teaspoon soy sauce

Per serving: Calories 48, Protein 2 g, Fat 0 g, Carbohydrates 8 g, Calcium 15 mg, Fiber 2 g, Sodium 38 mg

FRESH SHIITAKE PÂTÉ

This spread can be made with almost any kind of mushroom. Eat your fill and freeze the rest!

Yield: about 2 cups

1 tablespoon olive oil
1 cup chopped onion
1 clove garlic, pressed
½ lb. fresh shiitake mushrooms, chopped (about 4 cups)
1 tablespoon soy sauce
1 teaspoon savory
½ teaspoon thyme
¼ teaspoon nutmeg
⅛ teaspoon black pepper

Sauté the onion and garlic in the olive oil. When the onion starts to soften, add the shiitake, and cook over low heat about 5 minutes. Add the rest of the ingredients, and simmer about 10 more minutes over low heat.

Purée all the ingredients together in a food processor or blender. Serve hot or cold.

Per 2 tablespoons: Calories 20, Protein 1 g, Fat 1 g, Carbohydrates 2 g, Calcium 3 mg, Fiber 6 g, Sodium 63 mg

CURRIED DIP

Try this habit-forming dip with raw or steamed vegetables.

Yield: 1 ¾ cups

Combine the tofu, curry paste, and lemon juice in a food processor or blender until smooth and creamy. Fold in the cucumber.

½ lb. soft tofu
3 tablespoons commercially prepared curry paste
2 tablespoons fresh lemon juice
1 cup chopped cucumber

Per ¼ cup: Calories 26, Protein 2 g, Fat 1 g, Carbohydrates 2 g, Calcium 15 mg, Fiber 1 g, Sodium 16 mg

FIESTA DIP

This dip sounds too easy to be true—but don't you believe it! Served hot or cold, it makes a great topping for nachos. Create a hot layered appetizer by adding onion slices, pepperoncinis (see glossary), mushrooms, guacamole, and/or jalapeños.

Yield: 1 cup

Combine the salsa and tahini, and mix well.

½ cup tahini
½ cup salsa

Lite Fiesta Dip: For a reduced-fat version, mix together 6 tablespoons salsa, ¼ cup tahini, ¼ cup nutritional yeast flakes, and 2 tablespoons white miso.

Per 2 tablespoons: Calories 91, Protein 3 g, Fat 7 g, Carbohydrates 5 g, Calcium 63 mg, Fiber 2 g, Sodium 161 mg

HERBED OLIVE SPREAD

Olive lovers won't be able to get enough of this sensational spread.

Yield: 8 servings

1½ cups pitted Kalamata olives
3 tablespoons capers
½ teaspoon rosemary
½ teaspoon oregano
¼ cup olive or other oil

Process all the ingredients together in a food processor until coarsely ground. Serve with Italian or other crusty bread.

Per serving: Calories 108, Protein 0 g, Fat 12 g, Carbohydrates 1 g, Calcium 27 mg, Fiber 1 g, Sodium 349 mg

HOLY MOLY GUACAMOLE

Max out the flavor of all your Mex recipes by saying "so long" to sour cream and using this creamy avocado spread instead.

Yield: 4 servings

2 ripe avocados, peeled and pitted
Juice of 1 lemon (3 tablespoons)
1 clove garlic, minced
¼ teaspoon salt
Chili powder and cayenne pepper,
  to taste

Combine all of the ingredients in a food processor, and process until smooth.

Per serving: Calories 174, Protein 2 g, Fat 12 g, Carbohydrates 13 g, Calcium 19 mg, Fiber 4 g, Sodium 141 mg

HUMMUS

This Middle Eastern spread will become one of your favorite condiments. Serve with pita bread or sliced veggies.

Yield: 8 servings

Blend the chick-peas and lemon juice in a food processor or blender until smooth. Add the garlic, tahini, parsley, salt, and pepper, and continue blending until smooth. If the mixture is too thick, add water or some olive oil until the consistency is smooth but not runny. Sprinkle with paprika and serve with warmed pita bread wedges.

1 (16-oz.) can chick-peas, drained
Juice of 1 lemon
1 clove garlic, crushed
1 tablespoon tahini
Lots of fresh parsley, finely chopped
Salt and pepper, to taste
Paprika

Per serving: Calories 109, Protein 5 g, Fat 2 g, Carbohydrates 17 g, Calcium 58 mg, Fiber 4 g, Sodium 8 mg

SNACKS & APPETIZERS

ONION DIP

Try this simple tofu version of the dry onion soup mix dip with raw vegetables or chips.

1 (12.3 oz.) pkg. firm silken tofu (1½ cups)
1 (1-oz.) pkg. dry onion soup mix

Combine all the ingredients in a food processor or blender until creamy. Refrigerate overnight to let the flavors blend.

Per 2 tablespoons: Calories 24, Protein 2 g, Fat 1 g, Carbohydrates 2 g, Calcium 8 mg, Fiber 0 g, Sodium 189 mg

Green diets are lean diets: Approximately 300,000 Americans die of weight-related illnesses every year, making fat the number two cause of preventable deaths (smoking is number one). Vegetarian diets are typically 25 percent lower in fat than meat-based diets.

S N A C K S & A P P E T I Z E R S

PESTO DIP

This is a wonderful dip to serve before dinner; its lively taste will rev up your taste buds!

Yield: 1 ½ cups

Chop the garlic in a food processor. Add and chop the basil and parsley. Add the tofu, pine nuts, soy Parmesan, and olive oil, and blend until smooth and creamy.

2 cloves garlic
½ cup packed fresh basil leaves
¼ cup packed fresh parsley leaves
½ lb. soft tofu
3 tablespoons pine nuts or walnuts
2 tablespoons soy Parmesan
2 tablespoons olive oil

Per 2 tablespoons: Calories 47, Protein 2 g, Fat 3 g, Carbohydrates 1 g, Calcium 8 mg, Fiber 0 g, Sodium 25 mg

SOUTH-OF-THE-BORDER SALSA CUPS

These mini corn cups are also great filled with guacamole, refried beans, or any other festive Tex-Mex fare.

Yield: about 30 mini-cups

10 (6-inch) corn tortillas
Vegetable oil for brushing the tortillas
2 ripe mangoes
1 cup cooked black beans
3 green onions, finely chopped
2 jalapeño peppers, seeded and minced
2 teaspoons minced fresh gingerroot
½ cup chopped fresh cilantro
3 tablespoons lime juice
1 tablespoon brown rice syrup
Salt and cayenne pepper, to taste

Preheat the oven to 400°F. Using a cookie or biscuit cutter, cut the tortillas into 2-inch circles. Brush both sides of each circle with vegetable oil, and press the circles into miniature muffin tins. Bake the tortilla circles for 6 minutes, or until they are crisp. Let cool.

Peel the mangoes and dice them into ¼-inch pieces. Combine the mangoes with the remaining ingredients, and stir gently. Add additional lime juice, brown rice syrup, or salt, if needed. Place a heaping teaspoon of the salsa mixture into each corn cup.

Per mini-cup: Calories 41, Protein 1 g, Fat 0 g, Carbohydrates 9 g, Calcium 18 mg, Fiber 1 g, Sodium 13 mg

ELEGANT EGGPLANT CROSTINI

For an unforgettable appetizer, serve these crostini with non-alcoholic champagne, made by combining 1 quart of club soda and 12 ounces of frozen white grape juice concentrate (thawed).

Yield: 16 small crostini

Mix the garlic with half of the olive oil. Slice the bread on the diagonal into 16 pieces. Brush both sides of each slice with the garlic and oil mixture. Bake at 300°F until golden.

To prepare the eggplant, preheat the oven to 375°F. Mix the eggplant with the remaining oil, and roast until golden; let cool.

Combine the eggplant with the tomatoes, parsley, and basil, and season with salt and pepper.

Arrange the eggplant mixture on top of the bread slices, and serve.

TOP TIP: To peel tomatoes easily, try this simple trick. Place the tomatoes in boiling water for 30 seconds, then remove them with a slotted spoon, and immediately plunge them into cold water to stop the cooking process. Use a sharp paring knife to pull the skins off.

1 clove garlic, crushed
½ cup olive oil
1 loaf of thin, crusty bread
1 eggplant, diced
3 tomatoes, skinned, seeded, and diced
Handful of fresh parsley, chopped
6 basil leaves, finely shredded
Salt and pepper, to taste

SNACKS & APPETIZERS

Per crostino: Calories 144, Protein 3 g, Fat 7 g, Carbohydrates 15 g, Calcium 26 mg, Fiber 2 g, Sodium 114 mg

FRAGRANT FOCACCIA

There's nothing like focaccia warm from the oven. Although the dough takes some time to rise, the preparation work is virtually effortless.

Yield: 8 slices

SNACKS & APPETIZERS

1 tablespoon active dry yeast
1 cup warm water
1 tablespoon sweetener of choice
1 tablespoon olive oil
½ teaspoon salt
2 cups whole wheat pastry flour
1 cup unbleached white flour
½ cup seeded and chopped plum
   tomatoes
1 tablespoon finely chopped fresh
   basil
¼ cup finely chopped onions
1 clove garlic, finely minced
½ green pepper, finely chopped

Sprinkle the yeast over the warm water, and let it soften and dissolve for about 5 minutes. Beat in the sweetener, olive oil, and salt with a mixer or wooden spoon. Add the whole wheat pastry flour, then beat until the dough is smooth and elastic. Add the unbleached flour, then beat and knead until smooth and elastic. Cover the dough in a lightly oiled bowl, and let it rise in a warm place until double in bulk, about 45 minutes.

Preheat the oven to 450°F. Punch down the dough and knead briefly. Lightly oil a 12-inch round pizza pan. Roll and stretch the dough to fit the pan. Punch holes in the dough about every inch over the pan with the end of a wooden spoon or chopstick. Sprinkle the tomatoes, basil, onions, garlic, and green pepper over the top.

Let rise again about 15 minutes, then bake for about 12 minutes or until browned. Cut into wedges and serve.

Per slice: Calories 182, Protein 6 g, Fat 2 g, Carbohydrates 34 g,
Calcium 36 mg, Fiber 4 g, Sodium 138 mg

APPETIZER ROLLS

The following three recipes utilize phyllo dough, available in most supermarkets. Phyllo is a paper-thin pastry used in Middle Eastern baking.

JAMAICAN STUFFED PASTRIES

Stuffed pastries with a curried pastry crust are sold by street vendors all over Jamaica. The rich, spicy filling is irresistible!

Yield: 36 to 48 pastries

To make the filling, steam-fry the onions, jalapeños, and garlic in a large, heavy, nonstick or lightly oiled skillet until the onion is limp. Add the tomato and green onions. Steam-fry until most of the liquid has evaporated. Add the 2 teaspoons curry powder, salt, thyme, and allspice, and stir-fry for a minute. Add the reconstituted textured vegetable protein and the lemon juice or sherry, mix well, and allow to cool.

Heat the vegetarian broth with 1 teaspoon curry powder until the curry powder is dissolved. Set aside to cool completely. Follow the filling directions on p. 54.

Filling:
2 large onions, minced
2 tablespoons chopped pickled jalapeño peppers (or Scotch bonnet peppers)
2 cloves garlic, minced
1 large tomato, chopped
½ cup minced green onions
2 teaspoons curry powder
1 teaspoon salt
½ teaspoon dried thyme
¼ teaspoon ground allspice
1½ cups dry textured vegetable protein granules, reconstituted in 1 cup + 2 tablespoons boiling water with 2 tablespoons soy sauce
2 tablespoons lemon juice or dry sherry

1 cup vegetable broth
1 teaspoon curry powder
9 full sheets phyllo pastry

Per pastry: Calories 26, Protein 2 g, Fat 0 g, Carbohydrates 5 g, Calcium 11 mg, Fiber 1 g, Sodium 122 mg

SAVORY INDIAN SAMOSAS

Like most Indian appetizers, these crispy pastries are usually deep-fried, but phyllo pastry makes a fine (and much easier) substitute for fried dough. You might want to ration them, or they will disappear in minutes!

Yield: 36 samosas

Vegetable Filling:
2 medium onions, minced
1 tablespoon ground coriander
½ teaspoon ground cumin
¼ teaspoon cayenne pepper
½ lb. thin-skinned potatoes, cubed
1 (10-oz.) pkg. frozen peas, thawed
  and drained
⅓ cup chopped fresh cilantro or
  parsley
Salt, to taste

9 full sheets of phyllo pastry,
  thawed and kept covered
Soymilk for brushing tops

In a large, lightly oiled or nonstick skillet, steam-fry the onions until they are limp. Add the coriander, cumin, and cayenne, and steam-fry for one minute. Remove from the heat and add the cubed potatoes, thawed peas, and cilantro or parsley. Mix well and add salt, to taste. Allow to cool. Follow the directions for filling on p. 54.

Per samosa: Calories 29, Protein 1 g, Fat 0 g, Carbohydrates 6 g,
Calcium 5 mg, Fiber 1 g, Sodium 20 mg

S N A C K S & A P P E T I Z E R S

SPANIKOPITA ROLLS

The filling for these little pies is a bit unusual, containing such un-Greek ingredients as tofu, nutritional yeast, and miso! But these unconventional ingredients give the filling a rich, feta-like taste, which is what you expect from spanikopita.

Yield: about 48 rolls

Prepare the filling (you can do this a day or two ahead of time) by mixing the tofu, miso, yeast, and salt together very well in a large bowl. Use your hands, a potato masher, or a fork. Add the squeezed-dry, cooked or frozen spinach, the steam-fried green onions, and the dill, and mix well. Follow the directions for filling on p. 54.

Filling:
1½ lbs. medium-firm tofu, drained and crumbled
¼ cup light miso
2 tablespoons nutritional yeast flakes
1 teaspoon salt
3 (10-oz.) pkgs. frozen chopped spinach, thawed and squeezed dry, or 3 lbs. fresh spinach, cleaned, steamed, squeezed dry, and chopped (you can substitute nettles, chard, or other greens for all or part of the spinach)
1 bunch green onions, chopped and steam-fried until soft
2 tablespoons dried dillweed (or ½ cup fresh, chopped)

12 full sheets of phyllo pastry, thawed and kept covered
Soymilk for brushing tops

Per roll: Calories 38, Protein 3 g, Fat 1 g, Carbohydrates 5 g, Calcium 44 mg, Fiber 1 g, Sodium 80 mg

SNACKS & APPETIZERS

FILLING APPETIZER ROLLS

To fill the appetizer rolls, stack four sheets of phyllo together (use only three for Spanikopita Rolls), and cut into four 6 x 5-inch rectangles with a pair of kitchen scissors or a sharp knife. Repeat with the remaining phyllo. You should have 36 to 48 rectangles. Keep the phyllo well covered with plastic wrap while you work. Preheat the oven to 400°F.

For each roll, place about 3 tablespoons of filling in one corner of a rectangle of phyllo. Roll the filled corner toward the center, then fold in the left and right corners, like an envelope, then roll up again. Cover the filled roll with plastic wrap while you finish.

Place the filled rolls, seam side down, on nonstick or lightly oiled cookie sheets. Brush the tops with soymilk. Brush the tops of the Jamaican Stuffed Pastries with the vegetable broth mixture. Bake for 20 minutes, or until golden brown. Serve hot.

Raising animals for food accounts for more than half of all water used in the United States. In fact, an estimated 5,000 gallons of water is needed to produce just one pound of beef.

THRICE AS NICE SPICED NUTS

These spiced nuts go fast, so you'd better make all three!

Pecans:
2½ tablespoons dairy-free margarine
2 teaspoons dried rosemary
1¼ teaspoons seasoned salt
⅛ teaspoon dried basil
⅛ teaspoon cayenne pepper
2 cups pecan halves

Per tablespoon: Calories 55, Protein 1 g,
Fat 4 g, Carbohydrates 2 g,
Calcium 3 mg, Fiber 1 g, Sodium 64 mg

Cashews:
2½ tablespoons dairy-free margarine
1 teaspoon salt
½ teaspoon ground cumin
½ teaspoon ground coriander
¼ teaspoon cayenne pepper
2 cups whole cashews

Per tablespoon: Calories 62, Protein 1 g,
Fat 5 g, Carbohydrates 3 g, Calcium 5 mg,
Fiber 0 g, Sodium 78 mg

The directions for each type of spiced nuts are the same:

Preheat the oven to 325°F.

Melt the margarine in a small saucepan. Add the seasonings and stir well.

Spread the nuts in a shallow baking pan. Pour the margarine mixture over the nuts, and stir until they are thoroughly coated.

Bake the nuts for 10 to 15 minutes, stirring every few minutes. Drain the nuts on paper towels, and let them cool before serving.

Almonds:
1½ tablespoons dairy-free margarine
1½ tablespoons Veggie Worcestershire Sauce, p. 25
1 teaspoon garlic salt
¼ teaspoon cinnamon
¼ teaspoon chili powder
Dash of hot pepper sauce
2 cups blanched whole almonds

Per tablespoon: Calories 61, Protein 2 g,
Fat 5 g, Carbohydrates 2 g,
Calcium 25 mg, Fiber 1 g, Sodium 71 mg

TOP TIP: For a real party hit, combine your favorite spiced nut recipe with raisins, chopped dried apricots, pretzels, sunflower seeds, toasted pumpkin seeds, or any of your favorite munchies.

SNACKS & APPETIZERS

WINE-MARINATED DRIED TOMATOES

This delicious, fat-free dish is a great appetizer and works well as part of an antipasto platter.

½ cup light vegetarian broth mixed with 1 teaspoon cornstarch

3 oz. dried tomatoes

½ cup dry red wine (or balsamic vinegar, or a mixture)

2 cloves garlic, peeled and minced

1 teaspoon salt

1 bay leaf

½ teaspoon dried thyme or rosemary, or a sprig of fresh thyme or rosemary

¼ teaspoon dried basil, oregano, or marjoram

Freshly ground black pepper, to taste

Mix the broth and cornstarch in a small saucepan, and stir constantly over high heat until it thickens and clears. Mix in the remaining ingredients, and pour into a sterilized pint jar. Seal tightly and refrigerate. Shake the jar at least once a day. The tomatoes are ready when they are no longer chewy. Refrigerated, they will keep for about a month. Multiply the recipe as needed.

Per ¼ cup: Calories 48, Protein 1 g, Fat 0 g, Carbohydrates 8 g, Calcium 7 mg, Fiber 1 g, Sodium 272 mg

SNACKS & APPETIZERS

SOUPS

"As we talked of freedom and justice for all, we sat down to steaks. I am eating misery, I thought, as I took the first bite. And spit it out."
—Alice Walker

CLASSIC BORSHCH

This wonderfully colored soup is delicious hot or cold. Do your grating in a food processor to save time.

Yield: 4½ cups

3 cups water
2 cups grated beets
1 cup grated carrots
1 cup diced tomatoes
⅓ cup minced onions
1 bay leaf
2 cups shredded beet greens and/or cabbage
2 tablespoons fresh lemon juice
1 tablespoon sweetener of choice
½ teaspoon salt
⅛ teaspoon freshly ground black pepper

Bring the water to a boil, then add the beets, carrots, tomatoes, onions, and bay leaf. Simmer for about 5 minutes or until the vegetables are tender.

Add the greens, lemon juice, sweetener, salt, and black pepper. Simmer about 5 more minutes or until the greens are tender. Remove the bay leaf. Serve hot or cold.

Per cup: Calories 82, Protein 1 g, Fat 0 g, Carbohydrates 19 g, Calcium 38 mg, Fiber 4 g, Sodium 291 mg

S O U P S

GOLDEN VEGETABLE NOODLE SOUP

There's nothing like the comforting effect of this warm, fragrant soup. Children love it on a winter afternoon.

Yield: 6 servings

In a large pot, steam-fry the onion, celery, and garlic until tender. Add the hot water, split peas, turmeric, and bay leaf, and simmer for 1 hour. Add the rest of the ingredients, and cook just until the noodles are soft and the carrots are tender, adding pepper if you like. If you are fighting a cold, a dash of cayenne in this soup is just what the doctor ordered!

1 large onion, chopped
½ cup chopped celery (stalks and leaves)
1 clove garlic, minced
8 cups hot water
½ cup yellow split peas, rinsed
½ teaspoon turmeric
1 bay leaf
1 cup broken, thin whole wheat or soy pasta
1 cup frozen peas
½ cup chopped carrots
½ cup chopped fresh parsley
⅓ cup nutritional yeast flakes
1 tablespoon salt
½ tablespoon soy sauce

S
O
U
P
S

Per serving: Calories 159, Protein 9 g, Fat 0 g, Carbohydrates 29 g, Calcium 58 mg, Fiber 5 g, Sodium 1179 mg

HOT-SHOT SOUP

A shot of hot sauce makes this soup sizzle. The optional shot of vodka could set it on fire!

2 tablespoons olive oil
2 cups chopped yellow onions
1 cup minced celery
1 cup minced green bell pepper
1 (8-oz.) can whole tomatoes
6 cups tomato-vegetable juice
   cocktail (such as V-8 juice)
2 tablespoons hot sauce
Grated zest of 2 limes
Juice of 1 lime (2 tablespoons)
2 tablespoons Veggie
   Worcestershire Sauce, p. 25
Salt and pepper, to taste
Vodka (optional)
Grilled corn kernels
Guacamole (your favorite recipe or
   Holy Mole Guacamole, p. 44)

Heat the olive oil in a heavy stock pot. Add the onions, celery, and bell pepper, and cover. Cook, stirring occasionally, until the onions are translucent and the peppers are soft. (Add a little water if necessary to prevent the vegetables from sticking.) Add the tomatoes, vegetable juice, hot sauce, and lime zest, and bring to a boil. Reduce the heat and simmer for 15 minutes. Let cool slightly, then purée the soup in batches in a blender. Return to the heat and simmer for 10 more minutes. Add the lime juice, Worcestershire sauce, salt, and pepper and, if desired, a half-shot of vodka. Stir well.

Pour the soup into individual bowls, and garnish with grilled corn kernels and a dollop of guacamole.

TOP TIP: This soup is H-O-T stuff. If you like your food a little more mild-mannered, use less hot sauce, or let the soup mellow in the refrigerator overnight. Reheat before serving.

Per serving: Calories 131, Protein 3 g, Fat 6 g, Carbohydrates 19 g,
Calcium 54 mg, Fiber 2 g, Sodium 1110 mg

MAGNIFICENT MINESTRONE

Seek solace with this homey soup when the days are damp and chilly.

Yield: 11 cups

Preheat oven to 375°F.

Mix together the soy sauce and garlic powder, and squeeze into the tofu cubes. Bake the tofu on an oiled cookie sheet for 10 minutes. Turn the cubes and bake 5 minutes more. Set aside.

Sauté the onion, carrots, and zucchini in the olive oil for about 10 minutes. Combine the sautéed vegetables in a soup pot with the tomatoes, water, tomato juice, basil oregano, garlic powder, salt, and pepper. Bring to a boil and add the spaghetti. Simmer for 15 minutes, then add the kidney beans and browned tofu cubes.

Serve when the beans and tofu are heated through.

3 tablespoons soy sauce
½ teaspoon garlic powder
1 lb. tofu, frozen, thawed, squeezed out, and cut into ¾-inch cubes
1 medium onion, chopped
2 carrots, sliced
1 medium zucchini, sliced
2 tablespoons olive oil
1 (28-oz.) can tomatoes, chopped
4 cups water
2 cups tomato juice
2 teaspoons basil
1 teaspoon oregano
½ teaspoon garlic powder
½ teaspoon salt
¼ teaspoon pepper
3 oz. noodles or broken spaghetti
1 (15-oz.) can kidney beans

S O U P S

Per 1 cup serving: Calories 147, Protein 8 g, Fat 4 g, Carbohydrates 18 g, Calcium 83 mg, Fiber 4 g, Sodium 522 mg

THICK AND CREAMY ONION SOUP

The potatoes in this recipe add richness and body with a fraction of the fat in cream.

Yield: 6 servings

6 large onions, thinly sliced
¼ cup flour
1 teaspoon paprika
1 teaspoon salt
2 cups water
4 large potatoes, peeled and sliced
2 cups soymilk or rice milk
Pepper and additional salt, to taste
Paprika
Parsley (optional)

In a large, heavy pot, steam-fry the onions in a little water or broth until golden and soft. Stir in the flour, paprika, and salt. Add the water and blend well. Cover and simmer for 30 minutes.

Meanwhile, boil the potatoes in enough water to almost cover until tender. Mash the potatoes in whatever cooking water is left. Add the potatoes and soymilk to the onion mixture. Add the salt (if you prefer more) and pepper to taste. Heat gently and sprinkle each serving with paprika and/or chopped parsley.

TOP TIP: You can also use low-fat soymilk in this recipe and still get delicious results.

Per serving: Calories 178, Protein 4 g, Fat 1 g, Carbohydrates 38 g, Calcium 61 mg, Fiber 5 g, Sodium 374 mg

SOUPS

BODACIOUS BLACK BEAN CHILI

A hearty, low-fat version of a Southwestern favorite. Textured vegetable protein adds a "fooled-you" beefy texture.

Yield: 6 servings

In a large pot, sauté the onion and garlic in the oil until the onions become soft. Add the mushrooms and sauté for 5 minutes. Add the peppers and sauté for a few more minutes. Add the black beans, tomatoes, textured vegetable protein, chili powder, and salt, and simmer for ½ hour. Serve topped with nutritional yeast flakes or vegan sour cream.

1 large onion, chopped
2 cloves garlic, crushed
2-3 tablespoons olive oil
1 lb. mushrooms, sliced
1 green pepper, chopped
1 green chili pepper or jalapeño, chopped
1 (16-oz.) can black beans
1 (16-oz.) can crushed tomatoes
½ cup dry textured vegetable protein granules
Chili powder and salt, to taste
Nutritional yeast flakes (optional)
Vegan sour cream (optional)

S O U P S

Per serving: Calories 242, Protein 11 g, Fat 6 g, Carbohydrates 34 g, Calcium 65 mg, Fiber 8 g, Sodium 39 mg

CHIPOTLE SPLIT PEA SOUP

Chipotle is a smoked jalapeño pepper that adds a smoky flavor without the ham hock.

2 cups dried split peas
8 cups boiling water
1 medium onion, chopped
2 cloves garlic, minced
2 carrots, sliced diagonally
2 stalks celery, sliced diagonally
½ cup chopped parsley
½ chipotle, finely cut (1 teaspoon)
   or more, to taste
1 tablespoon low-sodium soy sauce

Simmer the split peas in the boiling water until soft, about 1 hour. Add the remaining ingredients and continue cooking until the vegetables are tender, adding more water as needed.

Per cup: Calories 107, Protein 6 g, Fat 0 g, Carbohydrates 20 g,
Calcium 28 g, Fiber 5 g, Sodium 105 mg

CREAMY POTATO LEEK SOUP

This soup is so thick and creamy, it's hard to believe there isn't a speck of artery-clogging cream in it!

Yield: 6 servings

In a large soup pot, boil the potatoes in the 8 cups water until cooked, about 10 minutes. Meanwhile, sauté the leeks and mushrooms in the margarine and ¼ cup water until soft, then add to the cooked potatoes. Crumble the tofu into the pot with your hands. Blend this mixture in a blender or food processor in batches until smooth and creamy. Return to the pot. Whisk in the vegetable broth powder, salt, and pepper to taste.

TOP TIP: To clean the leeks, cut the white part in half, and fan the layers with your fingers under running water.

2-3 potatoes, peeled and diced (about 4 cups)
8 cups water
2-3 leeks (white part only), diced
¼ lb. mushrooms, chopped (oyster if available, otherwise button)
2 tablespoons dairy-free margarine
¼ cup water
1 (12.3-oz.) pkg. firm or extra-firm silken tofu (1½ cups)
1½-2 tablespoons dry vegetable broth powder, or to taste
Salt and pepper, to taste

S
O
U
P
S

Per serving: Calories 203, Protein 6 g, Fat 6 g, Carbohydrates 31 g, Calcium 56 mg, Fiber 4 g, Sodium 209 mg

CREAMY TOMATO BISQUE

This bisque has a gourmet-meal taste, yet comes out of cans! Silken tofu blended with water makes an excellent base for creamy soups.

Yield: 4 servings

1 (12.3 oz.) pkg. firm silken tofu
  (1½ cups)
1 cup water
1 (10¾-oz.) can tomato soup
1 (14½-oz.) can low-sodium, diced
  tomatoes
¼ cup dry sherry
Dash of pepper

Blend the tofu and water until smooth. Combine all the ingredients and heat.

Per serving: Calories 170, Protein 7 g, Fat 3 g, Carbohydrates 23 g, Calcium 46 mg, Fiber 2 g, Sodium 637 mg

Eating soybeans saves animals! Over a lifetime, each vegetarian spares more than 2,400 animals from suffering and death.

DELECTABLE DAL SOUP

Take your taste buds on a trip around the world with this rich soup inspired by the flavors of India.

Yield: 4 servings

In a large pot, sauté the onions in the oil until tender but not browned. Add the garlic and spices, and cook for 1 minute. Add the mung beans and vegetable stock, and stir well. Bring the mixture to a boil, and simmer gently for 30 minutes, or until the beans are very tender. Stir occasionally to prevent the beans from sticking.

Cool the bean mixture slightly, place it in a food processor, and purée until smooth. Reheat the bean mixture, then divide it among 4 bowls. Sprinkle the toasted coconut on top, and serve.

2 medium onions, peeled and chopped
2 tablespoons olive oil
1 clove garlic
1 heaping teaspoon turmeric
1 teaspoon ground coriander
½ teaspoon paprika
½ teaspoon salt
½ lb. mung beans
4 cups vegetable stock
½ cup toasted, flaked coconut

SOUPS

Per serving: Calories 299, Protein 4 g, Fat 24 g, Carbohydrates 15 g, Calcium 38 mg, Fiber 5 g, Sodium 430 mg

HEARTY WINTER SQUASH-AND-POTATO SOUP

This thick, chunky soup is sure to warm your cockles on crisp fall afternoons.

1 large acorn or butternut squash
3-4 medium potatoes, peeled and
   cubed
1 tablespoon olive oil
1 large onion, finely chopped
2 cloves garlic, minced
Spices, to taste: thyme, sage, celery
   salt, parsley, salt, and pepper

Cut the squash in half, scoop out the seeds, and place cut side down in a shallow baking dish filled with ¼ inch water. Bake at 400°F for 45 to 60 minutes.

In a large pot, bring 3 cups of water to a boil. Add the potatoes, reduce the heat, and simmer for 20 minutes. Meanwhile, heat the olive oil in a small frying pan. Add the onion and garlic, and cook until the onion is clear. When the squash is done, scoop out the flesh and add to the potatoes and water. Mash with a potato masher until chunky, then add the onions and garlic. Add the spices to taste, and simmer for 20 minutes. If a thinner soup is desired, add more water. You can top each bowl with pumpkin seeds or sunflower seeds.

Per serving: Calories 223, Protein 3 g, Fat 2 g, Carbohydrates 45 g,
Calcium 86 mg, Fiber 8 g, Sodium 15 mg

SOUPS

MUSHROOM BARLEY SOUP

A pot of this fragrant soup simmering on the stove on a brisk winter day will warm you to the soul!

Combine all the ingredients except the barley and rice. Simmer over low heat for about 1 hour. Add the barley and rice, and simmer another ½ hour. (More water or broth may needed at that point.)

6 cups water or vegetable broth
2 onions, diced
2 potatoes, diced
2 stalks celery, diced
2 carrots, chopped
½ cup dried lima beans
¼ cup dried split peas
1 (14½-oz.) can chopped tomatoes
1 cup sliced mushrooms
1 tablespoon oil
Salt and pepper, to taste
½ cup barley
¼ cup rice

S
O
U
P
S

Per serving: Calories 181, Protein 5 g, Fat 2 g, Carbohydrates 34 g, Calcium 50 mg, Fiber 6 g, Sodium 35 mg

INCREDIBLE CREAM OF CELERY SOUP

This subtle, creamy soup is blended instead of strained, retaining all the vegetable fiber.

Yield: 5 cups

½ cup chopped onion (¼ lb.)
4 cups chopped celery (1 lb.)
2 cloves garlic, minced
½ tablespoon soybean or olive oil
2 cups vegetable stock or water
1½ teaspoons salt
¼ teaspoon dill
1 cup soymilk
Green onions, chopped (optional)
Fresh dill (optional)

Sauté the onion, celery, and garlic in the oil. Add the stock and simmer until soft.

Blend with a hand blender or in an electric blender until creamy. Return to the soup pot, stir in the salt, dill, and soymilk, and heat until almost boiling. Do not boil. Serve hot, garnished with chopped green onions or a sprig of fresh dill.

Per cup: Calories 48, Protein 2 g, Fat 2 g, Carbohydrates 5 g,
Calcium 44 mg, Fiber 2 g, Sodium 726 mg

S
O
U
P
S

WHITE CHILI

You're sure to get praised for this new twist on the Old West. Make it as spicy as you like!

Yield: 6 to 8 servings

Sauté the onion, garlic, and cumin in the oil until the onions are soft. Place all the beans with their liquid and the chilies in a casserole dish. Add the onion mixture and mix well. Cover and bake at 350°F for 45 minutes. Serve with hot sauce and salt and pepper to taste.

1 onion, diced
2 cloves garlic, minced
1 teaspoon cumin
1 tablespoon olive oil
1 (15-oz.) can of each with the
  cooking liquid:
  Chick-peas
  Hominy (white corn)
  Large butter beans
  Small navy beans
1 (4-oz.) can chopped mild green
  chilies
Salt and pepper, to taste
Hot sauce, to taste

Per serving: Calories 604, Protein 5 g, Fat 19 g, Carbohydrates 118 g, Calcium 115 mg, Fiber 29 g, Sodium 228 mg

EMILY

"Emily is no ordinary cow," reported the local papers. No, ordinary cows don't have names. Newspapers don't feature articles about them. Communities don't band together to save them. So, what made Emily special?

Emily spent most of her short life on a dairy farm, but, despite repeated attempts at artificial insemination, she never became pregnant. There is no room for a barren cow on the milk production line.

One cold New England morning, Emily was loaded onto a truck. Soon she found herself in a holding pen at Arena slaughterhouse. The smell of sweat and fear filled the air, and her sensitive nose surely recognized danger.

Freedom beckoned from beyond the 5-foot fence. Thinking only of escape, the brave bovine hurled her 1,400-pound frame over the barrier and fled for her life.

For weeks, the slaughterhouse workers tried to capture Emily, but she had learned to fear humans, with their loud, angry voices and fiery electric prods. Somehow, she managed to conceal herself in the backwoods, foraging for what little food she could find. Local residents heard of her plight and formed an "underground railroad," leaving bales of hay in the woods and refusing to report sightings of her to officials.

When Meg and Lewis Randa heard about Emily, they knew they had to help her. Their farm was already home to rescued horses, goats, rabbits, and dogs, and they determined that there was also room for a needy cow. They contacted the slaughterhouse owner, who agreed to sell the troublesome missing animal for $1.

The Randa family, assisted by an army of local supporters, set out to rescue the frightened cow, using succulent morsels of food and gentle coaxing voices. For days, she watched her rescuers but eluded them. Then, on Christmas Eve, a weak and thin Emily decided to trust again. She walked into the Randas' borrowed trailer and found herself being driven to her new home. The next day, Christmas dinner, featuring a delicious vegan stew—and top grade hay—was served in the barn to all the guests, including Emily.

The Randas say Emily has developed a fondness for bread, likes to have the top of her head scratched, and loves to kiss her new friends with her big cow tongue. People visit her and pet her and bring her gifts, some leaving notes pinned to the barn and the fence—messages of love and contrition. One read simply, "I used to eat cows. I'm sorry. No more."

AMAZING ANIMALS

SALADS
&
SALAD DRESSINGS

"I can't bear the idea of killing things. Fish seem to have as much right to stay alive as mice and warthogs. Never eat things with faces."
—Actress Joanna Lumley

ARTICHOKE HEARTS WITH FRESH BASIL

These artichoke hearts are easy to prepare and sublime to consume. They're perfect for summer.

Yield: 4 servings

1 (14-oz.) can artichoke hearts
¼ small red onion, diced
5 basil leaves, julienned
⅛ cup red wine vinegar
Salt, to taste

Cut the artichokes in half or quarters, and place in a small bowl. Add the diced red onion, basil leaves, red wine vinegar, and salt. Toss gently and serve.

Per serving: Calories 39, Protein 2 g, Fat 0 g, Carbohydrates 8 g,
Calcium 21 mg, Fiber 2 g, Sodium 47 mg

ASIAN PASTA

Chewy Oriental noodles, combined with the wonderful flavors of sesame oil and ume plum vinegar, will please even the most worldly palate.

Yield: 4 servings

½ lb. soba or udon noodles
3 tablespoons ume plum vinegar
3 tablespoons brown rice vinegar
3 tablespoons mirin
3 tablespoons sesame oil
¼-½ teaspoon crushed red pepper, to taste
1 red bell pepper, chopped
1 green bell pepper, chopped

Cook the pasta according to the package directions.

Meanwhile, place the ume plum vinegar, brown rice vinegar, mirin, sesame oil, and crushed red pepper in a jar with a tight-fitting lid, and shake to combine.

Drain the pasta and combine it with the bell peppers in a large bowl. Pour the dressing over the pasta, and toss to coat. Refrigerate for several hours or overnight, stirring occasionally. Serve chilled or at room temperature.

Per serving: Calories 319, Protein: 6 g, Fat 10 g, Carbohydrates 46 g,
Calcium 3 mg, Fiber 1 g, Sodium 2 mg

SALADS & SALAD DRESSINGS

"BEAT THE HEAT" BULGUR SALAD

Boiling water is as close as you'll come to cooking when making this refreshingly simple salad.

Yield: 6 servings

Pour the boiling water over the bulgur in a large bowl. Cover the bowl and let the bulgur set for 20 to 30 minutes. Fluff the bulgur with a fork, then let it cool to room temperature.

Stir the nuts, sunflower seeds, raisins, and chives into the bulgur. Toss the diced apple with the lemon juice. Add the apple-lemon juice mixture and the remaining ingredients to the bulgur mixture, and mix well. Serve immediately or chill until needed.

1 cup raw bulgur
2 cups boiling water
⅓ cup coarsely chopped toasted walnuts
⅓ cup coarsely chopped toasted pecans
¼ cup toasted sunflower seeds
½ cup golden raisins
2 tablespoons minced fresh chives
1 apple, cored and finely diced
1-1½ tablespoons lemon juice
2 tablespoons canola oil
¼-½ teaspoon cumin
¼ teaspoon cinnamon
Dash nutmeg

Per serving: Calories 304, Protein 6 g, Fat 14 g, Carbohydrates 36 g, Calcium 87 mg, Fiber 5 g, Sodium 7 mg

BOWTIE SURPRISE
WITH GRILLED GARDEN VEGGIES

You'll be surprised at how easy it is to perk up pasta salads with grilled vegetables. Feel free to try your favorite combination of veggies in this dish.

Yield: 6 servings

2 cups cooked red beans
2 tablespoons olive oil, plus more
   for brushing vegetables
2 tablespoons apple cider vinegar
½ lb. bowtie pasta
¼ cup chopped fresh parsley
Salt and pepper, to taste
⅓ cup Italian vinaigrette dressing,
   or to taste
1 small onion
3 large tomatoes
2 large zucchini
3 tablespoons chopped fresh basil

Mix together the beans, 2 tablespoons olive oil, and the vinegar, and refrigerate for several hours or overnight.

Cook the pasta, then drain and rinse it until cool. Toss the pasta with the bean mixture. Stir in the parsley, salt, pepper, and enough vinaigrette to moisten. Refrigerate until needed.

Parboil the onion. Cut the onion and tomatoes into quarters, and cut the zucchini into 1-inch chunks. Brush the vegetables with the remaining olive oil, and place on skewers. Grill, turning often, until lightly charred. Chop the vegetables, toss them into the pasta salad, add the basil, and serve.

Per serving: Calories 196, Protein 7 g, Fat 5 g, Carbohydrates 30 g,
Calcium 46 mg, Fiber 6 g, Sodium 114 mg

CRANBERRY SALAD

This is a variation on the traditional fruit salad. Perfect for summer barbecues, or as a refreshing alternative to canned cranberry sauce at Thanksgiving.

Yield: about 2 quarts

Chop the cranberries in a food processor, then add the sugar, and mix. Let stand for 2 hours. Cut the mandarin oranges in half. Add, along with the remaining ingredients, to the cranberries, mix well, and chill.

1 lb. cranberries
1½ cups sugar
1 (11-oz.) can mandarin oranges
1 small apple, finely chopped
¾ cup chopped nuts
1 (1-lb.) can crushed pineapple
   with ¼ cup of the juice
2 stalks celery, finely chopped

Per ¼ cup serving: Calories 313, Protein 2 g, Fat 6 g, Carbohydrates 61 g, Calcium 26 mg, Fiber 4 g, Sodium 15 mg

SALADS & SALAD DRESSINGS

FABULOUS FATOOSH

One taste of this version of fatoosh, the Middle Eastern bread salad, and your taste buds will declare it "Pita the Great!"

Yield: 4 servings

2 (6-inch) whole wheat pitas, dried until crisp*
1 large cucumber, peeled and diced
2 large ripe tomatoes, diced
3 scallions, thinly sliced
1 cup fresh finely minced parsley
⅓ cup finely minced fresh mint
2 cups cooked chick-peas (rinsed and drained, if canned)
¼ cup lemon juice
¼ cup olive oil
1 clove garlic, minced
½ teaspoon salt
¼ teaspoon black pepper
Kalamata olives for garnish (optional)

Tear the pita bread into 1-inch pieces, and set aside.

In a large bowl, combine the cucumber, tomatoes, scallions, parsley, mint, and chick-peas.

Place the lemon juice, olive oil, garlic, salt, and pepper in a jar with a tight-fitting lid. Shake until well mixed. Pour the dressing over the cucumber mixture, and toss to coat. Stir in the pita bread, and serve immediately on a bed of mixed greens, or chill the cucumber mixture for 1 hour and then add the pita bread just before serving. (If you chill the salad, you may need to adjust the seasonings.) Garnish with Kalamata olives, if desired.

*TOP TIP: Dry out the pita bread by leaving it uncovered at room temperature for about 6 hours. Or bake the bread at 400°F until it is lightly toasted, about 5 minutes.

Per serving: Calories 361, Protein 10 g, Fat 15 g, Carbohydrates 44 g, Calcium 115 mg, Fiber 9 g, Sodium 445 mg

GREAT GREEK SALAD

Zesty marinated tofu stands in for feta in this animal-friendly remake of the old deli classic.

Yield: 10 to 12 servings

Dressing:
¼ cup olive oil
2 tablespoons wine vinegar
1 teaspoon salt
1 teaspoon basil
½ teaspoon black pepper
¼ teaspoon oregano

1 lb. tofu, cut into ¾-inch cubes,
  or 1 recipe Frankly Fake Feta,
  p. 22
3 fresh tomatoes, cored and cut into
  wedges
3 cucumbers, thinly sliced
½ large red onion, chopped
½ cup Greek black olives
1 head leaf lettuce, washed and
  dried

Mix together the dressing ingredients, pour over the tofu, and marinate for at least 1 hour.

Add the tomatoes, cucumbers, onion, and olives to the tofu. Toss and serve on the lettuce.

Per serving: Calories 111, Protein 4 g, Fat 8 g, Carbohydrates 6 g, Calcium 77 mg, Fiber 2 g, Sodium 250 mg

JICAMA SALAD WITH ORANGE VINAIGRETTE

Don't be afraid of this exotic-sounding vegetable. It's really a mild-mannered tuber that makes a super salad.

Yield: 4 servings

1 cup orange juice
1½ tablespoons orange marmalade
4 cups jicama root, peeled and
    sliced into julienne strips
1 red bell pepper, diced
3 tablespoons chopped fresh
    parsley
Salt, to taste (optional)

Whisk together the orange juice and marmalade. Add the remaining ingredients and mix well. Marinate in the refrigerator several hours or overnight.

Per serving: Calories 104, Protein 2 g, Fat 0 g, Carbohydrates 24 g,
Calcium 11 mg, Fiber 1 g, Sodium 11 mg

MOCK CHICKEN SALAD

Yield: 4 cups

1 lb. tofu, cut into ½-inch cubes
2 tablespoons fresh lemon juice
½ teaspoon celery salt
1 cup diced celery
¼ cup minced green onions
½ cup slivered, toasted almonds
½ teaspoon salt
1 cup Tofu Sour Cream, p. 24

In a bowl, combine the tofu, lemon juice, and celery salt. Add the celery, green onions, almonds, and salt. Blend together with the Tofu Sour Cream. Chill and serve.

Per ½ cup: Calories 159, Protein 8 g, Fat 11 g, Carbohydrates 6 g,
Calcium 124 mg, Fiber 2 g, Sodium 381 mg

MUSHROOM SALAD WITH BALSAMIC VINEGAR

This is an uncomplicated recipe that puts mushrooms at center stage.

Yield: 6 servings

Bring the water to a boil, and add the mushrooms. Cook for 4 minutes, drain, and cool under cold running water. Combine with the remaining ingredients, and taste. Let the mushrooms marinate for 4 hours in the refrigerator. This salad is even better the next day.

1 qt. water
1 lb. mushrooms
⅜-½ cup balsamic vinegar
1 small red onion, diced

Per serving: Calories 24, Protein 1 g, Fat 0 g, Carbohydrates 4 g, Calcium 6 mg, Fiber 1 g, Sodium 2 mg

More than 260 million acres of U.S. forest have been cleared to grow crops needed to feed cattle, and another acre of trees disappears every eight seconds. Each vegetarian saves an acre of trees every year.

SALADS & SALAD DRESSINGS

NOODLES WITH PEANUT SAUCE

If you have a passion for peanut butter, you'll love this exotic—but easy—dish.

S A L A D S   &   S A L A D   D R E S S I N G S

½ lb. uncooked spaghetti
½ cup peanut butter
½ cup water
4 tablespoons soy sauce
1 teaspoon peeled, minced
  gingerroot
2 tablespoons brown rice syrup
2 tablespoons brown rice vinegar
1 teaspoon chili powder
Dash cayenne pepper
¼ cup chopped onion
Raisins

Cook the spaghetti according to the package directions.

Meanwhile, place the peanut butter and water in a large bowl, and whisk until smooth. Add the soy sauce, gingerroot, rice syrup, rice vinegar, chili powder, and cayenne pepper, and whisk.

When the spaghetti is done, rinse it with cold water, and drain. Add the spaghetti and onions to the peanut sauce, and toss well until the spaghetti is coated with the sauce. Refrigerate for several hours or overnight.

Before serving, toss the spaghetti again. Divide among 4 plates and sprinkle raisins over each serving.

Per serving: Calories 321, Protein 14 g, Fat 14 g, Carbohydrates 34 g,
Calcium 26 mg, Fiber 3 g, Sodium 1016 mg

PAPA PEDRO'S POTATO SALAD

Papas, mamas, and kids of all ages will love this delightfully different potato salad.

Cook the potatoes and cut into ½-inch cubes. Combine the oil, vinegar, sugar, chili powder, seasoned salt, and hot sauce, and pour over the warm potatoes. Cover and refrigerate for 1 hour. Add the corn, olives, onion, and green pepper, garnish with parsley, and serve.

5 large red potatoes
⅓ cup vegetable oil
¼ cup cider vinegar
1 tablespoon sugar
1½ teaspoons chili powder
1 teaspoon seasoned salt
⅛ teaspoon hot sauce
1 (8¾-oz.) can whole corn, drained
½ cup sliced black olives
1 small onion, thinly sliced
½ cup chopped green pepper
  (optional)
Parsley (for garnish)

Per serving: Calories 343, Protein 3 g, Fat 15 g, Carbohydrates 46 g,
Calcium 32 mg, Fiber 6 g, Sodium 393 mg

SALADS & SALAD DRESSINGS

PSYCHEDELIC PASTA SALAD

A rainbow of colors that tastes as good as it looks. Bring this gorgeous salad along to the company picnic, and watch it disappear!

Yield: 6 servings

1 (½-lb.) pkg. tri-colored pasta, cooked

3 ears corn, cooked, with the kernels cut from the cob

1 bunch broccoli florets, cut small and steamed

15 large black olives, sliced

15 green olives with pimento, sliced

1 (14-oz.) can artichoke hearts, halved

1 red pepper, diced

1 (8-oz.) can water chestnuts

1 (15-oz.) can chick-peas

⅓ cup of your favorite Italian dressing, or more to taste

Combine all the ingredients, mix well, and refrigerate. Serve cold.

Per serving: Calories 295, Protein 10 g, Fat 4 g, Carbohydrates 53 g, Calcium 97 mg, Fiber 11 g, Sodium 412 mg

RED-SKIN POTATO SALAD

You'll love the vinegary zing of this tangy version of the old classic. It's versatile enough to go from the picnic table to an elegant dinner party.

Yield: 6 to 8 servings

Bring the water to a boil in a large pot. Add the potatoes and cook until soft, about 8-10 minutes. Mix the olive oil, vinegar, garlic, mustard, and pepper. Drain the potatoes and pour the dressing over them. Let set 1 hour.

5 cups water
3 lbs. red potatoes, cut into
   bite-sized pieces
½ cup olive oil
½ cup red wine vinegar
2 cloves garlic, crushed
2 tablespoons Dijon mustard
Pepper, to taste

Per serving: Calories 314, Protein 2 g, Fat 15 g, Carbohydrates 40 g,
Calcium 16 mg, Fiber 4 g, Sodium 130 mg

SWEET-AND-SOUR CUKES

You might want to double the recipe—these pickles are known for their quick disappearing act!

Yield: 3 cups

½-1 teaspoon coarse salt (or
   substitute table salt, if necessary)
4 medium cucumbers, peeled and
   thinly sliced
1 medium onion, thinly sliced
½ cup sugar
½ cup white vinegar
¾ cup water

Sprinkle the salt over the sliced cucumbers, and let stand in the refrigerator for several hours. Drain the juice from the cucumbers, and rinse twice with cold water. Drain well.

Mix together the sugar, vinegar, and water, and add to the cucumbers along with the sliced onion. Place in a jar and let marinate in the refrigerator for several hours before serving. (They keep up to a week in the refrigerator.)

Per 2 tablespoons: Calories 24, Protein 0 g, Fat 0 g, Carbohydrates 6 g,
Calcium 9 mg, Fiber 1 g, Sodium 23 mg

TASTY "TOONA" SALAD

The whole family will love this "fab fake." Try it on a toasted bagel with lettuce and tomato for a tasty treat any time of the day.

Yield: 4 servings

Squeeze the excess moisture out of the thawed tofu, and crumble it into small pieces. Combine with the bell pepper, onion, and carrot.

Stir together the mayonnaise, soy sauce, lemon juice, and kelp powder in a small bowl. Add the mayonnaise mixture to the tofu and vegetables, and mix well.

*TOP TIP: Kelp and kombu powders, made from dried sea vegetables, give this salad a more authentic taste of the sea. But if you can't find them in your local health food store or Asian market, don't despair—this recipe will still taste terrific!

1 lb. frozen firm tofu, thawed
¼ small green bell pepper, finely chopped
1 tablespoon minced red onion
2 tablespoons grated carrot
½ cup egg-free mayonnaise
2 tablespoons soy sauce
1 tablespoon lemon juice
½-1 teaspoon kelp or kombu powder* (optional)

Per serving: Calories 166, Protein 9 g, Fat 11 g, Carbohydrates 6 g, Calcium 123 mg, Fiber 1 g, Sodium 172 mg

THAI COLE SLAW

This inexpensive and easy salad makes a great accompaniment to an Oriental meal or a perfect addition to a summer cookout.

Salad:
3 cups finely shredded cabbage (any type)
1 medium carrot, shredded
1 small onion, thinly sliced (preferably sweet)
2 tablespoons minced fresh cilantro or parsley
2 tablespoons minced fresh mint, or 2 teaspoons dried mint

Dressing:
2 tablespoons low-sodium soy sauce
2 tablespoons lime or lemon juice
2 tablespoons water or low-sodium vegetarian broth
1 tablespoon sugar or other sweetener
1 tablespoon slivered lime or lemon zest
Pinch of kelp powder (optional)

Mix the salad ingredients in a serving bowl, and add the dressing. Mix well and refrigerate until serving time.

Per serving: Calories 46, Protein 1 g, Fat 0 g, Carbohydrates 10 g, Calcium 38 mg, Fiber 2 g, Sodium 317 mg

BLEU "CHEESE" SALAD DRESSING

Sacre bleu! This low-fat dressing is almost too good to be true.

Yield: about 1 ½ cups

Combine all the ingredients in a blender until very smooth. If the dressing is too thick, add a little more water. Keep refrigerated in a covered jar.

TOP TIP: You can use low-fat tofu in this recipe and still get delicious results.

½ cup crumbled firm or medium-firm tofu
⅓ cup water
3 tablespoons lemon juice
2 tablespoons sesame meal
1 tablespoon vinegar (cider, white wine, or rice)
1 teaspoon salt, or 1 tablespoon white miso + ½ teaspoon salt
1 large clove garlic, crushed
¼ teaspoon white pepper
¼ teaspoon soy sauce or Veggie Worcestershire Sauce, p. 25

SALADS & SALAD DRESSINGS

Per 2 tablespoons: Calories 14, Protein 1 g, Fat 0 g, Carbohydrates 1 g, Calcium 14 mg, Fiber 0 g, Sodium 186 mg

CREAMY "BACON"-ORANGE DRESSING

Orange juice and "bacon" aren't just for breakfast any more. Add a little bit of the unexpected to your next salad with this tasty combination.

Yield: 1 cup

6 tablespoons freshly squeezed
   orange juice (from 1 large orange)
¼ cup soft or medium-firm tofu
¼ cup tofu mayonnaise
   (commercial, or see p. 23)
1½ tablespoons fresh lemon juice
1 tablespoon Dijon mustard
White bulbs of 3 green onions,
   chopped
1 teaspoon soy bacon bits or chips
1 teaspoon sugar or other
   sweetener
1 large clove garlic, peeled
½ teaspoon sesame oil
¼ teaspoon salt

Place all the ingredients in a blender, and process until creamy. Refrigerate.

Per 2 tablespoons: Calories 39, Protein 1 g, Fat 2 g, Carbohydrates 2 g,
Calcium 13 mg, Fiber 0 g, Sodium 175 mg

CREAMY DILL DRESSING

This low-fat topping makes anything it touches perfectly delightful.

Yield: about 2 cups

Combine all the ingredients in a blender until very smooth. If the dressing is too thick, add a little more water. To make a thicker dill dip, use less water.

TOP TIP: You can use low-fat tofu in this recipe and still get delicious results.

½ lb. medium-firm or firm tofu
½ cup water
¼ cup lemon juice
¼ cup fresh parsley
¼ cup chopped green onion
1 tablespoon chopped fresh dillweed, or 1 teaspoon dried dillweed
1 tablespoon chopped fresh basil, or 1 teaspoon dried basil
¼ teaspoon salt
¼ teaspoon sugar
1 clove garlic, crushed
Pinch cayenne

Per 2 tablespoons: Calories 13, Protein 1 g, Fat 1 g, Carbohydrates 1 g, Calcium 18 mg, Fiber 0 g, Sodium 35 mg

FAT-FREE SALAD SLIMMER

Use this easy combination in place of the oil in your favorite dressing recipes.

Yield: 1 cup

1 cup cold water or low-sodium
   vegetarian broth
2 teaspoons cornstarch

Cook, stirring constantly, over high heat until thickened and clear. It will thicken further when chilled.

Per tablespoon: Calories 1, Protein 0 g, Fat 0 g, Carbohydrates 0 g,
Calcium 0 mg, Fiber 0 g, Sodium 0 mg

POPPY SEED PASSION DRESSING

A low-fat dressing that's perfect on fruit salads—equally at home drizzled over orange and grapefruit sections or exotic fruits like mango and papaya. Be careful—it may be addictive!

Yield: about 1 ¾ cups

1 cup Fat-Free Salad Slimmer (see
   above)
6 tablespoons lemon juice
¼ cup maple syrup
1-2 tablespoons poppy seeds
½ teaspoon salt
1 teaspoon dry mustard
1 teaspoon paprika
1 teaspoon lemon zest

Combine all the ingredients in a covered jar, and shake.

Per 2 tablespoons: Calories 26, Protein 0 g, Fat 0 g, Carbohydrates 6 g,
Calcium 14 mg, Fiber 0 g, Sodium 77 mg

SENSATIONAL "SOY-ONNAISE" DRESSING

This mayonnaise substitute is low on fat, but high on flavor. It has a zippy bite that adds a zing to sandwiches and salads. It will keep in the refrigerator for up to a week.

Yield: 1 ¾ cups

Combine all the ingredients in a blender or food processor until smooth and creamy.

1 (12.3-oz.) pkg. firm silken tofu (1½ cups)
2 tablespoons + 1 teaspoon apple cider vinegar
1 tablespoon sugar or other sweetener
½ teaspoon salt
¼ teaspoon garlic powder
⅛ teaspoon dry mustard

Per 2 tablespoons: Calories 20, Protein 2 g, Fat 1 g, Carbohydrates 2 g, Calcium 7 mg, Fiber 0 g, Sodium 85 mg

TERRIFIC TARTAR SAUCE

When's the last time you had a tartar sauce that was good for you? This one's good for your finned friends too, when you serve it with Crispy Tofu Cubes, p. 113, Faux Fish Cakes, p. 114, or Un-Chicken Filet, p. 104.

Yield: 2 cups

1 (12.3 oz.) pkg. firm silken tofu
   (1½ cups)
2 tablespoons + 1 teaspoon lemon
   juice
2 teaspoons onion powder
½ teaspoon dry mustard
½ teaspoon salt
7 tablespoons chopped onion
3½ tablespoons sweet pickle relish

Combine the tofu, lemon juice, onion powder, mustard, and salt in a blender until smooth and creamy. Fold in the onion and pickle relish.

Thousand Island Dressing: Add ¼ cup ketchup when blending the ingredients together.

Per 2 tablespoons: Calories 20, Protein 2 g, Fat 1 g, Carbohydrates 2 g,
Calcium 8 mg, Fiber 0 g, Sodium 98 mg

SALADS & SALAD DRESSINGS

94

SANDWICHES

"Come to think of it, peanut butter and jelly doesn't seem too bad."
—ABC TV reporter after "interviewing" rescued turkeys

CHICK-PEA PITA POCKETS

This super spread takes just minutes to make and is sure to become a lunchtime favorite!

1 (16-oz.) can chick-peas, rinsed,
   drained, and mashed
⅓ cup chopped celery
1 tablespoon minced onion
2 tablespoons pickle relish
2 tablespoons egg-free mayonnaise
1 teaspoon mustard
Dash of garlic powder (optional)
4 whole wheat pitas
Lettuce, tomato slices, grated
   carrot, etc., for toppings

Place the chick-peas, celery, onion, pickle relish, mayonnaise, mustard, and garlic powder in a bowl, and stir well.

Cut the pitas in half, and open up into pockets. Fill each pita pocket with ⅛ of the chick-pea spread, top with lettuce, tomato slices or other veggies, and serve immediately. For bag lunches, pack the spread, veggies, and pita bread in separate containers, and assemble just before eating.

Per serving: Calories 357, Protein 14 g, Fat 4 g, Carbohydrates 65 g, Calcium 101 mg, Fiber 11 g, Sodium 556 mg

A cow grazing on one acre of land produces enough meat to feed one person for two and a half months. Soybeans grown on that same acre would produce enough protein to feed someone for seven years.

SANDWICHES

DEVILED TEMPEH SPREAD

This spicy spread is so devilishly good, you'd think we'd made a deal with you-know-who. Whether served on crackers for a snack or spread on a sandwich for lunch, it's a heck of a good treat!

Yield: 1 ½ cups

Steam the tempeh for 20 minutes.

Process all the ingredients in a food processor until smooth and spreadable.

½ lb. tempeh
1 tablespoon ketchup
1 tablespoon miso
1 teaspoon onion powder
½ teaspoon garlic powder
½ teaspoon sage
½ teaspoon thyme
⅛ teaspoon cracked red pepper

Per ¼ cup serving: Calories 92, Protein 8 g, Fat 4 g, Carbohydrates 8 g, Calcium 38 mg, Fiber 2 g, Sodium 168 mg

Sandwich Tips

Move over, peanut butter and jelly! Sandwich fillings can be just about anything you have on hand:

- *Stuff a sandwich roll with lettuce, tomato, veggie deli slices like vegetarian bologna or vegetarian turkey, and a sliver of nondairy cheese.*
- *Try this quick veggie wrap—Stuff tortillas with your choice of: sprouts, lettuce, green onions, tomatoes, avocado, grated zucchini, grated carrot, olives, and soy cheese. Drizzle with balsamic vinegar, lemon juice, and olive oil, and roll up.*

- *Salsa, horseradish, mustard, barbecue sauce, salad dressings, guacamole, and other creative condiments give any sandwich a kick.*
- *Dress up a bagel with tofu cream cheese, all-fruit preserves, and nut butters.*
- *Melt soy cheese over whatever veggies you have in the refrigerator.*
- *Perk up peanut butter by mashing with bananas, berries, or applesauce.*
- *Hold everything together with bagels, tortillas, pitas, or chapatis.*

ITALIAN EGGPLANT SANDWICH

Turn your kitchen into a New York deli with this zesty Italian sub. Molto buono!

Yield: 2 sandwiches

S
A
N
D
W
I
C
H
E
S

1 eggplant
½ cup soymilk
Egg replacer, equivalent to 1 egg
Kosher salt, to taste
1 cup flour
1 cup vegan Italian-style bread
  crumbs
Olive oil, as needed
2 sub rolls, sliced in half
½ cup marinara sauce
Vegan cheese

Preheat the oven to 350°F.

Peel and slice the eggplant into ¼-inch slices, and set aside. Combine the soymilk, egg replacer, and a pinch of salt (if desired), and mix well. Set up a breading station with one bowl for each: flour, egg replacer mixture, and bread crumbs. Dredge the eggplant in the flour, and shake off the excess. Submerge it in the egg replacer mixture, shake off the excess, then coat evenly with bread crumbs. Pan-fry the eggplant until golden on both sides.

Finish in the oven for about 6 minutes. Remove from the oven and place on the sliced sub rolls. Add the marinara sauce and vegan cheese, and serve immediately.

Per sandwich: Calories 641, Protein 26 g, Fat 10 g, Carbohydrates 111 g,
Calcium 348 mg, Fiber 8 g, Sodium 951 mg

"MEATY" MUSHROOM SANDWICHES

Grilled veggie sandwiches are a summertime staple for many vegetarians. If you don't have a grill, broil the veggies in your oven instead.

Yield: 4 servings

Put the vinegar, garlic, salt, pepper, and 4 tablespoons olive oil in a small jar, and shake well. Set aside.

Clean the mushrooms and remove their stems. Brush the vegetables with olive oil. Grill the mushrooms for 3 to 4 minutes on each side. Place the onion and tomato chunks on skewers and grill, turning often, until lightly charred. Cut each mushroom in half, and cut the onion and tomato chunks into thin slices.

Spread a little of the vinegar mixture on each slice of bread, then top with the mushrooms, onions, tomatoes, and basil leaves.

TOP TIP: To make mushrooms even "meatier," buy them four or five days before you plan to grill them. Clean the mushrooms and allow them to dry out in a paper bag in your refrigerator.

2½-3 teaspoons balsamic or red wine vinegar
1 large garlic clove, minced
Salt and pepper, to taste
4 tablespoons olive oil, plus more for brushing the vegetables
2 large portobello mushrooms
1 red onion, cut into chunks
1 tomato, cut into quarters
8 slices crusty Italian bread
Basil leaves

Per serving: Calories 319, Protein 7 g, Fat 13 g, Carbohydrates 40 g, Calcium 24 mg, Fiber 3 g, Sodium 358 mg

NO-BLUES BBQ

If you've been blue because you've missed the taste of down-home barbecue sandwiches, this easy recipe will have you smiling again!

Yield: 4 servings

1 lb. extra-firm tofu
1 cup barbecue sauce
4 whole wheat sandwich rolls
Sandwich fixin's: sautéed onions,
   diced bell peppers, etc.

SANDWICHES

TOP TIP: Blue because you don't like barbecue? Tofu can also be marinated in sweet and sour sauce, spicy salsa, or red pepper pesto—or brushed with a little olive oil and dusted with your favorite dry seasoning mix. Baked marinated tofu can be used in everything from salads and sandwiches to stir-fries and stews.

Drain the tofu and cut it in half horizontally to make two pieces. Wrap the tofu in a clean towel, press it between two baking sheets with a heavy weight on top, and refrigerate for an hour or more.

Unwrap the tofu and place it in a shallow baking dish. Spoon ¾ cup of the barbecue sauce over the tofu, cover the baking dish, and let the tofu marinate in the refrigerator for at least several hours. The longer the tofu marinates (up to five days), the more flavorful it will be.

Place the marinated tofu on a lightly oiled baking sheet, and bake at 400°F for 1 hour. Slice the sandwich rolls open, cut the tofu into thin slices, and divide it among the rolls. Mix the sautéed onions, bell peppers, or your favorite fixin's with the remaining barbecue sauce, and spoon over the sandwiches.

Per serving: Calories 300, Protein 14 g, Fat 5 g, Carbohydrates 47 g,
Calcium 165 mg, Fiber 3 g, Sodium 1290 mg

NOUVEAU SLOPPY JOE

Old Sloppy Joe: Lots of fat, not too nice to cows. Nouveau Sloppy Joe: A cow's (and your heart's) best friend. One thing they have in common: Finger lickin' good!

Yield: 4 servings

Steam the tempeh for 20 minutes, and cut into ¼-inch cubes.

To microwave, cook the onion, green pepper, and garlic in 2 tablespoons water in a 1-quart microwave-safe container for 1 minute on HIGH. Stir in the tempeh, Marinara Madness, chili powder, and salt, and cook on HIGH for about 2 more minutes or until heated through.

To cook on top of the stove, simmer the onion, green pepper, and garlic in ¼ cup water until the vegetables are soft. Stir in the tempeh, Marinara Madness, chili powder, and salt, and simmer until heated through.

Serve on toasted buns.

½ lb. tempeh
1 onion, chopped
1 green pepper, chopped
2 cloves garlic, minced
2 cups Marinara Madness, p. 18
2 teaspoons chili powder
½ teaspoon salt
4 buns, toasted

S
A
N
D
W
I
C
H
E
S

Per serving: Calories 275, Protein 15 g, Fat 4 g, Carbohydrates 42 g, Calcium 136 g, Fiber 8 g, Sodium 763 mg

RICE PATTIES

Wondering what to do with that leftover rice from last night's stir-fry? Here's the answer—brawny, beefless burgers, loaded with flavor, not fat.

½ cup wheat germ
½ cup peeled, chopped plum
   tomatoes
2 cups cooked brown rice or other
   cooked grain
1 cup uncooked rolled oats
½ teaspoon garlic
1 small onion
1-2 tablespoons nutritional yeast
½ teaspoon salt
1 tablespoon oil

Mix together all the ingredients, except the oil.

Form into 9 burgers and brown on a nonstick griddle with nonstick cooking spray, or grill using 1 tablespoon oil. Serve on buns with all the fixin's.

Per burger: Calories 131, Protein 5 g, Fat 2 g, Carbohydrates 21 g,
Calcium 17 mg, Fiber 3 g, Sodium 121 mg

TEX-MEX TORTILLA ROLL-UPS

Brown-baggers: You can turn lunchtime into a fiesta if you remember to pack these portable Tex-Mex treats.

Yield: 4 servings

Place the beans, lime juice, orange juice, garlic, salt, and cayenne pepper in a food processor, and blend until smooth. Spoon the mixture into a bowl, and mix in the scallions and bell peppers.

Spread one-fourth of the mixture on each tortilla. Roll the tortillas tightly and wrap them in aluminum foil or plastic wrap. Chill the rolls several hours or overnight.

To serve, slice the tortillas crosswise into ½-inch rounds, and top with salsa.

2 cups cooked black beans (rinsed and drained, if canned)
2 tablespoons lime juice
2 tablespoons orange juice
2 garlic cloves, coarsely chopped
⅛ teaspoon salt
Cayenne pepper, to taste
3 scallions, finely chopped
¼ cup finely chopped red or green bell pepper
4 (6-inch) flour or corn tortillas
Salsa

Per serving: Calories 202, Protein 9 g, Fat 2 g, Carbohydrates 37 g, Calcium 33 mg, Fiber 5 g, Sodium 181 mg

UN-CHICKEN FILET

This versatile patty makes a smashing sandwich—or a mouthwatering main dish. Serve on a sourdough roll with sliced apples, mustard, and lettuce, or dress it up like traditional chicken dishes—such as cacciatore or Southern style with mashed potatoes and gravy.

Yield: 6 (3-inch) burgers

1 lb. tofu
¼ cup wheat germ
¼ cup whole wheat flour
2 tablespoons nutritional yeast
1 tablespoon grated onion
½ teaspoon garlic powder
½ teaspoon poultry seasoning
¼ teaspoon black pepper
1 tablespoon oil

In a bowl, mix and mash together all the ingredients except the oil, and form into 3-inch burgers. Brown each side in the oil. Serve hot on a bun, either plain or with all the fixin's.

Per burger: Calories 119, Protein 8 g, Fat 6 g, Carbohydrates 9 g, Calcium 86 mg, Fiber 2 g, Sodium 9 mg

MAIN DISHES

copyright Peter Max 1997

"I come from cattle country. That's why I became a vegetarian."

—k.d. lang

ARTICHOKE TOFU PASTA

Some people believe this pasta has magical properties. You be the judge!

Yield: 4 servings

½ lb. tri-colored pasta (or elbow macaroni)
½ medium onion, chopped
2 cloves garlic
1 tablespoon olive oil
¼ lb. firm or extra-firm tofu, diced
1 (14-oz.) can artichoke hearts, quartered
1 (12-oz.) can diced tomatoes
1 (8-oz.) can tomato sauce

Cook the pasta according to the package directions. While the pasta is cooking, sauté the onion and garlic in the olive oil for 1 to 2 minutes. Add the diced tofu and sauté for 2 minutes, then add the artichokes, tomatoes, and tomato sauce. Drain the pasta and combine all the ingredients.

Per serving: Calories 222, Protein 7 g, Fat 5 g, Carbohydrates 36 g, Calcium 101 mg, Fiber 8 g, Sodium 475 mg

MAIN DISHES

"BEEFLESS" STEW

Remember the old-fashioned beef stew your mom used to make? Well this vegan version is even better! Serve it to your mom, and see if she doesn't agree.

Yield: 6 servings

Reconstitute the beef-style chunks in the boiling water and lemon juice. Let stand for 5 to 10 minutes. Brown the onion and garlic in the oil, add the chunks, and continue browning. Add 4 cups water, the tomatoes, Worcestershire sauce, bay leaves, salt, pepper, allspice, bouillon cube, and sugar, and simmer for one hour. Add the carrots, potatoes, and peas. Cook another 30 minutes. Thicken with the cornstarch.

1 cup dry "beef"-style textured vegetable protein chunks
⅞ cup boiling water
1 teaspoon lemon juice
1 medium onion, chopped
1 clove garlic, minced
1 tablespoon oil
4 cups water
1 (14-oz.) can tomatoes
1 teaspoon Veggie Worcestershire Sauce, p. 25
2 small bay leaves
2 teaspoons salt
½ teaspoon pepper
Pinch ground allspice
1 vegetable bouillon cube
1 teaspoon sugar
6 carrots, chopped
3 potatoes, cut into bite-sized pieces
1 (10-oz.) pkg. frozen peas
2 tablespoons cornstarch, dissolved in a small amount of water

Per serving: Calories 217, Protein 11 g, Fat 2 g, Carbohydrates 38 g, Calcium 90 mg, Fiber 8 g, Sodium 760 mg

BEEFY SEITAN ROAST

This is excellent hot or sliced cold for sandwiches. Make the whole recipe and use the leftovers for sandwiches, or grind some in a meat grinder or food processor for "hamburger." Cut some of it into strips for stir-fries and stroganoff, and/or cut thicker slices for "steaks" or "cutlets" to pan-fry, grill, or broil (with or without a breading and with or without a grilling sauce, barbecue sauce, or marinade). Use the leftover cooking broth to enhance sauces.

Yield: 6 to 8 servings

2 cups instant gluten powder (vital wheat gluten)
2 tablespoons nutritional yeast flakes
1 teaspoon onion powder
½ teaspoon garlic granules
Black pepper, to taste

1½ cups cold water, or broth from soaking Chinese dried mushrooms
2 tablespoons ketchup
2 tablespoons soy sauce
2 teaspoons Marmite or other yeast extract, or dark miso
2 teaspoons browning and seasoning sauce (such as Kitchen Bouquet, etc.)

4 cups water or broth from soaking dried Chinese mushrooms
¼ cup ketchup
¼ cup soy sauce
4 teaspoons Marmite or other yeast extract, or dark miso
4 teaspoons browning and seasoning sauce

In a mixing bowl, mix the gluten powder, nutritional yeast, onion powder, garlic, and black pepper together. In a smaller bowl, whisk together the first batch of cold water or mushroom broth, ketchup, soy sauce, yeast extract, and browning sauce.

Pour the broth into the gluten mixture, and knead it into a ball. Place the ball into a roasting pan with a cover large enough to allow the ball to double in size (press the ball down to flatten a bit).

Preheat the oven to 350°F. Prepare a cooking broth made by mixing together the remaining ingredients. Pour over the gluten ball, and bake uncovered for ½ hour. Prick the roast all over with a fork, and turn it over. Lower the heat to 300°F, cover, and bake for 1 more hour, turning occasionally.

Slow-Cooker Method: Cook in a slow-cooker on HIGH for 10 hours.

Per serving: Calories 181, Protein 34 g, Fat 1 g, Carbohydrates 9 g, Calcium 14 mg, Fiber 0 g, Sodium 998 mg

BUTTERNUT AND CHESTNUT HOLIDAY SAUTÉ

Seasonal chestnuts add a special touch to this savory squash dish.

Drain the soaked lentils and cover with fresh water. Bring to a boil and cook until the lentils are tender, about 30 minutes. Heat the oil in a large sauté pan, and cook the shallots and garlic until just tender. Add the squash and cook for a few minutes. Add the tomatoes and thyme, and cook for 10 minutes. Add the lentils and cook for 10 more minutes or until all the ingredients are tender. Add the chestnuts and warm through. Serve with crusty bread.

1 cup dried lentils, soaked overnight
6 tablespoons olive oil
4 shallots, chopped
1 large garlic clove, minced
1 large butternut squash (about 1½ lbs.), peeled, seeded, and cut into cubes
1 lb. tomatoes, chopped and peeled, or 1 (16-oz.) can diced tomatoes
½ teaspoon chopped fresh thyme
1 cup shelled chestnuts

MAIN DISHES

Per serving: Calories 442, Protein 12 g, Fat 20 g, Carbohydrates 52 g, Calcium 107 mg, Fiber 11 g, Sodium 21 mg

CHICKEN-FRIENDLY TOFU NUGGETS
WITH MAPLE-MUSTARD DIPPING SAUCE

Say "so long" to fast-food chicken nuggets—animal-friendly tofu nuggets are better for you and the birds! These also taste great dipped in barbecue sauce, salsa, or spicy peanut sauce.

Yield: 4 servings

3 tablespoons all-purpose flour
6 tablespoons ice water
½ cup lightly toasted bread crumbs
1 teaspoon salt
Dash of cayenne pepper
Vegetable oil for frying
1 lb. firm or extra-firm tofu, pressed, frozen, thawed, and cut into 1-inch cubes

In a small bowl, whisk the flour and water together to make a smooth batter; in a separate dish, toss the bread crumbs with the salt and cayenne pepper.

Heat 1 inch of oil in a heavy skillet.

Dip each tofu cube in the batter to coat, then roll the cubes in the bread crumb mixture. Drop the cubes into the hot oil, and cook for 2 minutes. Turn the cubes and continue cooking until they are golden brown. Drain the cubes on paper towels, and serve immediately with Maple-Mustard Dipping Sauce

Maple-Mustard Dipping Sauce:
1½ teaspoons cornstarch
6 tablespoons water
¼ cup Dijon mustard
4 teaspoons maple syrup
1 teaspoon brown rice vinegar
1 teaspoon soy sauce

Dissolve the cornstarch in a small amount of the water. Place the cornstarch mixture in a small saucepan, and add the remaining water, along with the rest of the ingredients. Heat the sauce, stirring constantly, until thickened.

Per serving: Calories 199, Protein 10 g, Fat 8 g, Carbohydrates 20 g, Calcium 154 mg, Fiber 1 g, Sodium 1138 mg

CHICK-PEA CURRY

A delicious one-dish meal fit for a Maharaja—or your mother-in-law. The ample size can be halved for single cooks, or made in its entirety and frozen for quick meals on busy weeknights. (Our taste-testers say it's even better the second time around!)

Yield: 8 to 10 servings

Sauté the onions in the margarine. When golden brown, add the tomato sauce, garlic, and spices, and stir-fry for a few minutes. Add the chick-peas and the green pepper, and fry over fairly high heat until everything is browned, about 5 to 10 minutes. Add salt to taste, turn the heat down, add ½ cup water, and cover. Stir frequently and simmer for up to an hour. Serve over rice.

2½ medium onions, thinly sliced
½ cup dairy-free margarine
1 (8-oz.) can tomato sauce
8 cloves garlic, minced
2 teaspoons turmeric
1 teaspoon cumin
1 teaspoon allspice
1½ teaspoons cayenne pepper
½ teaspoon ginger
4 (15-oz.) cans chick-peas, drained
1-2 green bell peppers, cut into small pieces (optional)
Salt, to taste
½ cup water

Per serving: Calories 426, Protein 15 g, Fat 13 g, Carbohydrates 59 g, Calcium 115 mg, Fiber 12 g, Sodium 299 mg

COMFORTING KNISHES

This is classic comfort food—perfect for dreary winter days or whenever you need a pick-me-up.

Yield: 15 to 18 knishes

Dough:
1 cup mashed potatoes
1 tablespoon oil
1 teaspoon salt
3 cups unbleached white flour, or
   1½ cups whole wheat flour and
   1½ cups unbleached white flour
1 teaspoon baking powder
½ cup cold water

Filling:
1 cup chopped onions
2 tablespoons oil
1½ cups mashed potatoes
1½ cups mashed tofu
¼ cup chopped fresh parsley
1 teaspoon salt
½ teaspoon garlic powder
¼ teaspoon black pepper

Prepare 2½ cups mashed potatoes. To make the dough, beat together 1 cup of the mashed potatoes, the 1 tablespoon oil, and the salt. Add the flours and baking powder, and mix well. Mix in the water and knead into a smooth dough. Let rest on a board, covered with a cloth, for ½ hour.

To make the filling, sauté the onions in the 2 tablespoons oil until transparent. Mix together with the rest of the filling ingredients.

Cut the dough into 4 sections, then roll each section as thin as possible (about ¹⁄₁₆ inch thick). Cut into 5 x 6-inch rectangles. Place 2 or 3 tablespoons of filling in the middle of each rectangle. Fold the sides in first, then the ends.

Place folded side down on an oiled cookie sheet. Bake at 350°F for 25 minutes, or until golden. Serve with horseradish or mustard.

Per knish: Calories 136, Protein 4 g, Fat 3 g, Carbohydrates 22 g, Calcium 67 mg, Fiber 1 g, Sodium 262 mg

MAIN DISHES

CRISPY TOFU CUBES

Toss with fried rice or steamed rice with green onions for a quick and easy Oriental entrée. This recipe can also be prepared with thin slices of tofu instead of cubes for a tasty sandwich filling.

Yield: 4 servings

Cut the tofu into ¼-inch cubes. Do not pat dry.

Combine the nutritional yeast, flour, garlic salt, and pepper in a container with a lid. Add the tofu. Put the lid on the container, and shake well to coat the tofu.

Heat the oil in a nonstick skillet. Add the tofu and cook over medium heat, turning the tofu every few minutes until golden brown and crispy.

1 lb. firm tofu
3 tablespoons nutritional yeast
2 tablespoons flour
1 tablespoon garlic salt
1 teaspoon pepper
1-2 tablespoons oil

Per serving: Calories 126, Protein 7 g, Fat 8 g, Carbohydrates 7 g, Calcium 84 mg, Fiber 0 g, Sodium 1550 mg

FAUX FISH CAKES

These "cakes" are very tasty, with a mild seafood flavor, and they are a good way to use up that last two cups of leftover cooked rice. The plain ones make great "fish burgers," served on buns, but try the exotic flavor options on the next page as well. Freeze any leftovers (the uncooked mixture or the cooked patties) for future meals.

Yield: 20 cakes

1 lb. medium-firm tofu, frozen, thawed, well-squeezed, and finely crumbled
2 cups cooked short grain brown rice
1 small onion, minced
6 tablespoons nutritional yeast flakes
2 tablespoons minced celery
¼ lb. firm tofu
2½ tablespoons soy sauce
2 tablespoons water
1 tablespoon lemon juice
1 tablespoon herbal salt, or 2 tablespoons light miso
1 teaspoon kelp powder
½ teaspoon each dry mustard and dillweed
¼ teaspoon white pepper
Pinch celery seed
¼ cup unbleached flour or instant gluten flour (vital wheat gluten)

Mix the frozen tofu, rice, onion, yeast, and celery in a large bowl. Combine the remaining ingredients (except the flour) in a blender or food processor until smooth. Add this to the bowl, along with the flour. Mix well with your hands. (You can make this ahead of time and refrigerate it until you are ready to cook the patties.)

Form 20 thin patties and cook in a nonstick skillet over medium-low heat about 6 minutes per side, covering the skillet while cooking the first side.

Or place the patties on lightly greased or nonstick cookie sheets, and bake at 400°F for 7 minutes per side. The mixture can also be shaped like "fish sticks," if you like, instead of patties.

Serve "fish cakes" alone or on buns or toast with Terrific Tartar Sauce (p. 94), ketchup, or chili sauce.

Thai "Fish Cakes": Add 1 tablespoon Thai red chili paste, 4 cloves crushed garlic, and ½ cup chopped green beans or peas to the tofu-rice mixture. Top with a vinegar sauce made by mixing ½ cup vinegar, ⅓ cup minced onion, 2 tablespoons sugar, 2 tablespoons minced fresh basil or cilantro, 2 tablespoons grated carrot, and 1 small dried red chili, crushed.

Indian-Style "Fish Cakes": Add 2 tablespoons grated fresh gingerroot, 2 tablespoons minced cilantro, 1 tablespoon minced fresh mint, 2 cloves of garlic, crushed, and a pinch each of curry powder, cayenne, turmeric, coriander, and red chili pepper flakes to the tofu-rice mixture.

Jamaican-Style "Fish Cakes": Add 2 tablespoons chopped jalapeño and 2 teaspoons paprika to the tofu-rice mixture.

Cajun-Style "Fish Cakes": Add ½ cup minced green onion, 2 teaspoons Cajun seasoning, and 2 cloves of garlic, crushed.

TOP TIP: Using low-fat tofu in these recipes will still give delicious results.

Per cake: Calories 56, Protein 4 g, Fat 1 g, Carbohydrates 7 g, Calcium 39 mg, Fiber 1 g, Sodium 337 mg

FIRE-UP-THE-GRILL FAJITAS

Summer veggies sizzle in this marvelous Mex meal. Grill an extra ear of corn, and you'll have a great garnish for the Hot-Shot Soup, p. 60.

Yield: 4 servings

Juice of 2 limes (4 tablespoons)
1 tablespoon olive oil
1 clove garlic, minced
1 jalapeño pepper, seeded and minced (for extra heat, don't seed the pepper before mincing it)
2 tablespoons minced fresh cilantro
2 teaspoons chili powder
¼ teaspoon cayenne pepper (or more if you can stand it)
1 lb. extra-firm tofu, cut into 1-inch strips
2 ears fresh corn
1 large red onion
1 red bell pepper, cut into 1-inch squares
1 green bell pepper, cut into 1-inch squares
12 cherry tomatoes
4 large flour or corn tortillas
Guacamole (your favorite recipe or Holy Moly Guacamole, p. 44)

Put the lime juice, olive oil, garlic, jalapeño pepper, cilantro, chili powder, and cayenne pepper in a jar with a tight-fitting lid, and shake well. Put the tofu in a shallow pan, add the lime juice mixture, and marinate in the refrigerator, stirring occasionally, for several hours.

Meanwhile, remove the husks from the corn, and soak it in cold water for 1 hour. Drain the corn and wrap in aluminum foil. Grill for 20 to 30 minutes, turning often, until the corn is lightly charred. Cut the corn kernels off the cob.

Parboil the onion and cut into quarters. Thread the onion, bell peppers, and tomatoes onto skewers, and brush with some of the lime marinade. Grill, turning often, until lightly charred.

Place the tofu on the grill, cover with a lid or aluminum foil, and cook, basting occasionally with the marinade until the tofu is light brown.

Heat each tortilla briefly on the grill. Divide the vegetables and tofu equally among the tortillas, then roll them up fajita-style. Serve with guacamole.

Per serving: Calories 264, Protein 12 g, Fat 9 g, Carbohydrates 31 g, Calcium 138 mg, Fiber 5 g, Sodium 158 mg

Try these tips to make veggie-grilling more thrilling:

- Parboil or steam onions, potatoes, and other hard veggies before grilling them with softer ones. Cut all vegetables roughly the same size for even cooking.

- For heartier fare, grill seitan (wheat meat), tempeh, or extra-firm tofu along with your veggies. Tofu and tempeh will be more flavorful if they're marinated for at least one hour before grilling.

- Use a wire mesh grilling screen to prevent soft foods, like tofu and tomatoes, from falling into the fire.

- Grilled veggies perk up pizzas, pasta salads, pita pocket sandwiches—you name it! Be creative!

Americans are giving beef the boot—and replacing it with broccoli! In the past two decades, beef consumption has dropped 21 percent, while consumption of broccoli has soared 520 percent.

FUNNY-FACE BURRITOS

You'll want kids to play with their food when you prepare these silly burritos! They're great for a casual weekend supper.

Yield: 4 servings

4 large whole wheat tortillas
1 teaspoon canola oil
¼ yellow onion, diced
Chili powder to taste (optional)
1 (16-oz.) can kidney or pinto
   beans, rinsed and drained
¼ cup mild salsa

Toppings:
Sliced black olives
Cherry tomatoes
Red bell pepper strips
Cooked corn kernels
Shredded lettuce leaves
Grated carrots

Wrap the tortillas in foil, and warm them in the oven for about 10 minutes.

Meanwhile, heat the oil in a skillet over medium heat. Sauté the onion until softened, about 5 minutes. Add the chili powder and cook for 1 minute. Add the beans and salsa, and cook until the beans are heated through.

Place the bean mixture in a food processor, and purée until smooth.

Spread ¼ of the bean mixture on each tortilla. Let your kids make faces on the tortillas using the vegetables: for instance, sliced black olives for eyes, a cherry tomato for the nose, red pepper slices for lips, corn kernels for teeth, and shredded lettuce or grated carrots for hair.

Per serving: Calories 243, Protein 11 g, Fat 2 g, Carbohydrates 42 g,
Calcium 35 mg, Fiber 7 g, Sodium 263 mg

GENTLE SHEPHERD'S PIE

Traditional "shepherd's pie" is made with beef—but now a kind-hearted shepherd has stepped in and replaced the meat with hearty lentils. We think it's a change for the better—and so do the cows.

Yield: 4 servings

Rinse the lentils and pick over for small rocks. Boil the lentils, bay leaf, and garlic cloves in the 3 cups water for about 45 minutes until soft. Add additional water if necessary. With the side of a spoon, mash the garlic cloves against the side of the pan, and mix thoroughly with the lentils. Remove the bay leaf and season with salt and pepper.

While the lentils are cooking, boil the cubed potatoes for 10 to 15 minutes until soft. Drain and add the soymilk and margarine. Mash and beat by hand or with an electric mixer until fluffy. Season with salt and pepper.

To assemble the Gentle Shepherd's Pie, press the lentil mixture into the bottom of 9 x 12-inch baking dish. Cover with the mashed potatoes (like icing a cake). Bake in a pre-heated 350°F oven for 20 to 30 minutes until the potatoes start to get slightly brown and crusty.

1 cup dry green lentils
3 cups water
1 bay leaf
3 cloves garlic
Salt and pepper, to taste
2 large baking potatoes, peeled and cubed (about 4 cups)
Water as needed to boil
1 cup soymilk
1 tablespoon dairy-free margarine

MAIN DISHES

Per serving: Calories 325, Protein 13 g, Fat 4 g, Carbohydrates 59 g, Calcium 39 mg, Fiber 7 g, Sodium 51 mg

HOT AND SPICY LO MEIN

Kim chee, a traditional Korean condiment made with Chinese cabbage, daikon radish, and lots of hot pepper, is the key ingredient in this recipe. It is an extremely hot food. Kim chee can be found in some supermarkets in the produce section, but the best kim chee is found in Oriental markets.

Yield: 1 serving

1 single serving cup instant vegan Oriental-flavored soup noodles
½ cup kim chee with liquid, chopped
¼ lb. firm tofu, cubed
1 stalk (including white bulb) green onion, chopped

Cook the noodles in boiling water as directed on the label. Chop the kim chee. When the noodles are soft, pour into a serving bowl. Stir in the chopped kim chee with liquid and cubed tofu. Sprinkle with the chopped onion.

Per serving: Calories 293, Protein 14 g, Fat 6 g, Carbohydrates 46 g, Calcium 128 mg, Fiber 1 g, Sodium 338 mg

MAIN DISHES

JERK TEMPEH OR TOFU

Jerk is a Jamaican way of spicing food that usually involves the use of very hot peppers. A prepared jerk sauce can be used, or try the one below, and adjust the heat to your own taste. Scotch bonnet peppers are the ones used in Jamaica, but they are extremely hot on the hot pepper scale. A little jalapeño works for hot pepper wimps.

Yield: 4 to 6 servings

Combine all the ingredients together (except the scallions and tempeh or tofu) in a blender.

Cut the tempeh or tofu into 1-inch cubes or ½-inch strips, and arrange them one layer deep in a glass pan. Pour the blended mixture over the tempeh or tofu. Press the sauce into the tempeh or tofu with a spatula or the palms of your hands. Let marinate for a few hours or overnight.

Preheat the oven to broil, prepare the coals in the grill, or heat the griddle.

Broil for about 5 minutes, turn the tempeh or tofu over, and broil 5 more minutes. If you are cooking on a grill or oiled griddle, brown on both sides. Serve hot with chopped scallions for a garnish.

¼ cup apple or papaya juice
3 tablespoons grated onion
3 cloves garlic, minced
2 tablespoons soy sauce
2 tablespoons minced fresh hot
   pepper of your choice
2 tablespoons vinegar
1 tablespoon oil
1 tablespoon grated gingerroot
1½ teaspoons allspice
½ teaspoon cinnamon
½ teaspoon freshly ground black
   pepper
½ teaspoon thyme
¼ teaspoon nutmeg
1 lb. steamed tempeh or tofu
   frozen, thawed, and squeezed dry
½ cup chopped scallions

Per serving (with tempeh): Calories 222, Protein 18 g, Fat 9 g, Carbohydrates 19 g, Calcium 98 mg, Fiber 5 g, Sodium 409 mg

Per serving (with tofu): Calories 110, Protein 7 g, Fat 7 g, Carbohydrates 5 g, Calcium 109 mg, Fiber 1 g, Sodium 410 mg

LUCKY LUAU KEBABS

Pineapple and pork are commonly paired in Hawaiian fare, but you can enjoy the taste of the islands with these pig-friendly kebabs. Colorful kebabs served over pasta or rice make any get-together more festive. Grill at least four or five different vegetables, along with tempeh, tofu, or another "mock meat," and allow two full skewers per guest. Aloha!

MAIN DISHES

Tempeh
Teriyaki sauce (about 1 cup per pound of tempeh, plus more for brushing the kebabs)
Button mushrooms
Sweet potatoes
Walla Walla onions (or other sweet onions)
Fresh pineapple, cut into 1-inch chunks
Red and green bell peppers, cut into 1-inch squares
Cooked brown rice

Steam the tempeh for 15 minutes, then let it cool. Cut the tempeh in half lengthwise, then cut it into 1½-inch pieces. Pour the teriyaki sauce into a shallow container, and add the tempeh pieces. Marinate in the refrigerator, stirring occasionally, for at least 1 hour.

Meanwhile, trim any rough ends from the stems of the mushrooms. Steam the sweet potatoes until just done, let cool, then cut into 1-inch chunks. Parboil the onions, then cut into quarters. Soak wooden skewers in water for at least 15 minutes to keep them from burning.

Alternately thread the tempeh, mushrooms, sweet potatoes, onions, pineapple, and peppers on skewers. Brush with teriyaki sauce and grill for about 10 minutes, turning several times to cook evenly. Serve over brown rice.

MAGNIFICENT "MEATY" LASAGNE

This luscious lasagne contains neither meat nor dairy. But wait before you tell your guests—see if they can taste the difference first.

Yield: 8 to 12 servings

To prepare the tofu filling, blend all the ingredients in a food processor or blender until smooth.

To prepare the textured vegetable protein filling, pour the boiling water over the textured vegetable protein granules, and let stand for about 10 minutes. Meanwhile, sauté the onion, green pepper, garlic, basil, and oregano in the olive oil. Add the hydrated granules and soy sauce, and stir-fry for a few minutes.

Preheat the oven to 350°F. To assemble the lasagne, cook the lasagne noodles according to the directions on the package, and drain. Spread 1 cup Marinara Madness over the bottom of a 9 x 13-inch pan. Cover the sauce with 4 cooked lasagne noodles, and spread the tofu filling evenly over the noodles. Cover with 4 more cooked lasagne noodles and about 1½ cups sauce, then spread the textured vegetable protein filling evenly over the layer of sauce. Cover with 4 more cooked lasagne noodles, and the rest of the sauce, then cover evenly with the grated soy mozzarella cheese.

Cover and bake for about 30 minutes, then uncover for the last 5 minutes of baking.

Tofu Filling:
¾ lb. firm tofu
½ tablespoon onion powder
½ teaspoon salt
½ teaspoon basil
¼ teaspoon garlic powder

Textured Vegetable Protein Filling:
⅞ cup boiling water
1 cup textured vegetable protein granules
1 teaspoon olive oil
1 onion, chopped
1 green pepper, chopped
2 cloves garlic, minced
1 teaspoon basil
½ teaspoon oregano
1 tablespoon soy sauce

4 cups Marinara Madness, p. 18
12 uncooked lasagne noodles (½ lb.)
4 oz. soy mozzarella cheese, grated (optional)

TOP TIP: You can use low-fat tofu and soy cheese and still get delicious results.

Per serving: Calories 214, Protein 12 g, Fat 2 g, Carbohydrates 35 g, Calcium 84 g, Fiber 4 g, Sodium 438 mg

MAIN DISHES

123

MOUSSAKA

Moussaka is one of the first ways that North Americans become acquainted with eggplant, usually in a Greek restaurant. Unfortunately, although the dish is scrumptious, it is full of fatty meat and olive oil and topped with a rich, savory custard sauce made of egg yolks.

Our version is still delicious, but the eggplant is broiled instead of fried in olive oil (eggplant soaks up oil like a sponge!); textured vegetable protein supplies the bulk in a savory tomato sauce flavored with wine, mushrooms, cinnamon, and oregano; and a creamy, light sauce based on potatoes tops the casserole.

Yield: 8 servings

Tangy Cream Sauce:
1½ cups water
1 medium potato, peeled and cut into chunks
½ medium onion, peeled and cut into chunks
1 teaspoon salt, or 1 tablespoon light miso + ½ teaspoon salt
¼ lb. firm or medium-firm tofu, crumbled
4 tablespoons nutritional yeast flakes
1 tablespoon ground sesame seeds or sesame meal
1 tablespoon lemon juice
Pinch of garlic granules
Soy Parmesan (optional)

4 large eggplants (peeled, if desired), thinly sliced

To prepare the Tangy Cream Sauce, place the water, potato, onion, and salt (but not miso, if using) in a small pot, and bring to a boil. Cover and lower the heat to a good simmer. Cook until the potato is tender. Place this (along with all the liquid and miso, if using) in a blender or food processor with the remaining ingredients, and blend until very smooth. Set aside.

Place the eggplant slices on a nonstick or lightly oiled cookie sheet, and broil them in batches about 4 inches from the heat until slightly charred on each side and soft in the middle. Set aside.

To make the tomato sauce, steam-fry the onions and garlic in a large, nonstick or lightly oiled pot, until beginning to soften and brown. Add the mushrooms and steam-fry until the liquid evaporates. Add the remaining sauce ingredients, and simmer for about 20 minutes. Add a bit of water if it's too thick (but it should be thicker than spaghetti sauce). Add salt and pepper to taste. (If you want a "meatier" taste, use soy sauce instead of salt.)

Preheat the oven to 375°F.

To assemble the casserole, in a nonstick or lightly oiled, 9 x 13-inch casserole or baking pan, spread one-third of the tomato sauce. Layer half of the eggplant slices over this, then another third of the tomato sauce, then the remaining eggplant. Spread the last third of tomato sauce over the eggplant. Dribble the Tangy Cream Sauce over the top, and spread it evenly. Sprinkle it lightly with nutmeg.

Bake the casserole for 45 minutes, and let stand for 15 minutes before cutting.

Tomato Sauce:
5 large onions, minced
6 large cloves garlic, minced
1 lb. fresh mushrooms, chopped
2 cups dry textured vegetable protein granules, soaked in 1⅔ cups boiling water and ¼ cup soy sauce
2 (6-oz.) cans tomato paste
2 cups water
⅔ cup dry red wine
¼ cup fresh parsley, chopped
1 tablespoon dried oregano
2 teaspoons dried basil or rosemary
½ teaspoon freshly ground black pepper
¼ teaspoon ground cinnamon
Small bay leaf

Salt and black pepper, to taste
Freshly grated nutmeg

Per serving: Calories 287, Protein 17 g, Fat 1 g, Carbohydrates 46 g, Calcium 144 mg, Fiber 12 g, Sodium 325 mg

NEAT LOAF

Where's the beef? It's not in this tasty tofu loaf, which beats a mundane meat loaf any day of the week.

1 lb. firm tofu, mashed
½ cup wheat germ
⅓ cup chopped fresh parsley,
 or 1½ tablespoons dried parsley
¼ cup chopped onion,
 or 1 tablespoon onion powder
2 tablespoons soy sauce
2 tablespoons nutritional yeast
 (optional)
½ tablespoon Dijon mustard
¼ teaspoon garlic powder
¼ teaspoon black pepper
2 tablespoons oil

Preheat the oven to 350°F.

Mix together all the ingredients except the oil. Use the oil to coat a loaf pan. Press the tofu mixture into the oiled loaf pan, and bake for about 1 hour. Let cool about 10 minutes before removing from the pan. Garnish with ketchup and parsley. This is also good sliced and fried for sandwiches the next day.

Per serving: Calories 120, Protein 8 g, Fat 8 g, Carbohydrates 7 g,
Calcium 74 mg, Fiber 1 g, Sodium 323 mg

MAIN DISHES

NUTTY ZUCCHINI LOAF

Nut loaves make easy, yet elegant, entrées for any special occasion. Dinner guests will love the touch of coconut in this exotic dish.

Yield: 4 to 6 servings

Preheat the oven to 400°F.

Gently sauté the onions in 3 tablespoons of the olive oil. Add the garlic, cumin, coriander, and ginger, and cook for 30 seconds, stirring well.

In a separate pan, cook the zucchini in the remaining oil until just brown. Combine the onion mixture, zucchini, and the remaining ingredients. Press the mixture into an oiled ovenproof dish, and bake for 30 minutes.

Serve with a large salad of mixed greens.

2 onions, finely chopped
4 tablespoons olive oil
1 clove garlic, crushed
½ teaspoon cumin seeds
1 teaspoon ground coriander
1 teaspoon fresh, grated gingerroot, or ¼ teaspoon dried ginger
2 lbs. zucchini, diced
¾ cup chopped almonds
¾ cup chopped walnuts
¾ cup oatmeal
⅓ cup coconut milk
½ cup dried, flaked coconut
1 teaspoon salt
Pepper, to taste

Per serving: Calories 621, Protein 12 g, Fat 48 g, Carbohydrates 31 g, Calcium 139 mg, Fiber 9 g, Sodium 449 mg

QUICK STROGANOFF

Serve this delicious "meaty" stroganoff over hot pasta, rice, or mashed potatoes. Start cooking these first, because the stroganoff is very quickly made. Serve with a salad on the side.

1 large onion, thinly sliced
½ lb. white button mushrooms, sliced
2 cups slivered seitan or grilled portobello, boletus, or porcini mushrooms
2 tablespoons tomato paste
3 tablespoons dry sherry plus 3 tablespoons water, or ⅓ cup dry white wine (or non-alcoholic alternative)
1 (1-oz.) pkg. vegetarian dried onion soup mix
2 cups boiling water
1 teaspoon dry mustard
¾ cups Tofu Sour Cream, p. 24

In a large, nonstick skillet, steam-fry the onion and white mushrooms until the onion starts to soften. Add the seitan or grilled mushroom slivers, and stir-fry for a few minutes. Add the tomato paste along with the sherry and water or wine.

Dissolve the soup mix in the boiling water, and add to the pan with the wine and mustard. Simmer over medium-low heat for 5 minutes.

Add the Tofu Sour Cream to the pan over low heat, stirring gently until heated through. Serve immediately.

Variation: Instead of seitan or mushrooms, you can use slices of firm vegetarian "burger" or marinated firm tofu.

For extra flavor, add the tomato paste to the onion and mushrooms, and stir over medium heat until the paste starts to brown. Then add the seitan or mushroom slivers.

Per serving: Calories 210, Protein 22 g, Fat 6 g, Carbohydrates 14 g, Calcium 51 mg, Fiber 2 g, Sodium 602 mg

PIZZA TIPS

Pizza toppings are limited only by your imagination! Here are some quick ideas.

- Chop up whatever veggies are on hand, and drizzle some olive oil or crushed tomatoes over them.

- Try new ideas for toppings like crumbled tofu, sun-dried tomatoes, beans, spinach, or even corn.

- Add different sauces like pesto or red pepper and garlic purée, or no sauce at all.

- Get creative with fake meats— slice up some veggie bacon or pepperoni substitute.

- Try nutritional yeast for a great cheesy taste.

- Merge two cultures for a tasty Mexican pizza—refried beans, tomatoes, and salsa on an unbaked crust!

ROASTED VEGGIE PIZZAS

An easy way to bring out intense flavors in even the most mild-mannered veggies is to roast them. A tip for grill-less gourmets: You can substitute roasted veggies for grilled in almost any recipe.

Yield: 4 servings

Preheat the oven to 425°F.

Combine the eggplant, zucchini, onion, bell peppers, oil, vinegar, thyme, and pepper in a large baking dish, and toss to mix well. Bake, stirring occasionally, for 20 minutes, or until the vegetables are tender. Set aside.

Place the pizza shells on baking sheets. Spread about 2 tablespoons of the tomato sauce on each pizza shell, then top with the roasted vegetables. Bake for 10 to 12 minutes or until the pizza shells and vegetables are heated through.

1 small eggplant, sliced
1 medium zucchini, sliced
1 red onion, cut into small wedges
1 red bell pepper, thinly sliced
1 yellow bell pepper, thinly sliced
1 tablespoon olive oil
1 tablespoon balsamic vinegar
½ teaspoon dried thyme
¼ teaspoon black pepper
4 individual pizza shells
½ cup tomato sauce

Per serving: Calories 245, Protein 7 g, Fat 3 g, Carbohydrates 46 g, Calcium 72 mg, Fiber 9 g, Sodium 594 mg

SHERRIED PORTOBELLOS

This versatile dish can be served as is, tossed with pasta, poured over a baked potato, sautéed with veggies, or used in place of beef or steak strips in favorite recipes. Served over crusty bread, it also makes a mean "roast beef" sandwich.

Yield: 4 servings

2 (6-oz.) pkgs. sliced portobello
   mushrooms
2 teaspoons oil
2 cloves garlic, crushed
1-2 cups cooking sherry
Salt and pepper, to taste

Clean the mushrooms, wiping off any excess dirt around the stems. Sauté the garlic in the oil until light brown. Add the mushrooms and sherry. Cook until the mushrooms shrink, then add salt and pepper to taste.

Per serving: Calories 155, Protein 1 g, Fat 2 g, Carbohydrates 7 g,
Calcium 12 mg, Fiber 1 g, Sodium 12 mg

Ninety percent of the protein in plant foods, as well as 99 percent of the carbohydrates and 100 percent of the fiber, is wasted by feeding grain to livestock instead of to people.

SMOKY SPUDS AND BBQ BEANS

If you've never tried sweet potatoes and black beans together, you're in for a treat! This filling dish will cure all your cravings for barbecue.

Yield: 4 servings

Scrub the potatoes and cut them crosswise into thin slices. Brush with oil and grill for 15 to 20 minutes, turning the potatoes over once.

Meanwhile, combine the black beans and barbecue sauce in a medium saucepan. Simmer over very low heat to keep the beans warm while you're grilling the potatoes.

Top the potatoes with the hot black beans, and serve.

4 sweet potatoes
Vegetable oil for brushing the potatoes
2 cups cooked black beans
¾ cup barbecue sauce

Per serving: Calories 331, Protein 8 g, Fat 0 g, Carbohydrates 74 g, Calcium 51 mg, Fiber 8 g, Sodium 703 mg

STIR-FRIED TOFU AND VEGETABLES IN GINGER SAUCE

You'll swear by this marinade after one taste.

Yield: 4 to 6 servings

¾ cup soy sauce
¾ cup lemon juice
1-2 teaspoons grated fresh
  gingerroot
1 lb. extra-firm tofu
2 tablespoons vegetable oil
1 cup cauliflower florets
1 cup broccoli florets
3 carrots, cut into 2-inch strips
1 medium onion, sliced
1 green pepper, sliced
1 cup snow peas
1 cup sliced mushrooms
2 green onions, chopped
2 cups cooked rice

Mix the soy sauce, lemon juice, and ginger. Cut the tofu into 1-inch chunks, and place in the marinade. Let marinate for 45 minutes. Drain the tofu, saving the marinade. Heat the oil in a large pan, and add the cauliflower, broccoli, carrots, onion, green pepper, and tofu. Stir frequently, cooking evenly. Add the snow peas, mushrooms, and green onions. Continue to stir frequently until the vegetables are cooked but still crunchy. Serve over rice, topped with the marinade.

Per serving: Calories 299, Protein 14 g, Fat 9 g, Carbohydrates 37 g,
Calcium 166 mg, Fiber 6 g, Sodium 2450 mg

STUFFED ROASTED POBLANOS

Poblano peppers can range from very mild to definitely picante, so beware when you bite into them. The peppers can be roasted and peeled the day before and refrigerated or even frozen until ready for use.

Yield: 6 servings

Preheat the oven to broil.

Always handle hot peppers with rubber gloves (disposable ones are handy). Wash the peppers, then roast them under the broiler, turning them until charred and blistered all over. Close the blistered peppers in a plastic or paper bag for about 15 minutes, then remove the peels, membranes, and seeds. Slit the peppers open down one side.

Turn the oven down to 350°F.

Chop the garlic in a food processor, add the cilantro leaves, and chop. Add the lime juice, salt, and tofu, and blend until creamy. Stuff each pepper with about ⅓ cup of the tofu filling. Arrange the stuffed peppers in an 11 x 7-inch baking dish. Pour the tomato sauce over the peppers, and bake 35 to 40 minutes.

TOP TIP: You can use low-fat tofu and still get delicious results.

6 poblano peppers
2 cloves garlic
2 cups fresh cilantro leaves, lightly packed
3 tablespoons fresh lime juice
1 teaspoon salt
1 lb. firm tofu
1 cup tomato sauce

MAIN DISHES

Per serving: Calories 98, Protein 7 g, Fat 4 g, Carbohydrates 10 g, Calcium 123 mg, Fiber 3 g, Sodium 619 mg

SUMMERY STUFFED PEPPERS

These colorful, no-cook peppers, stuffed with a savory couscous salad, are just the thing when summer's heat has you beat.

Yield: 6 servings

½ cup uncooked couscous
1 cup boiling water
3 whole red bell peppers
3 whole yellow bell peppers
½ cup diced red bell peppers
½ cup diced yellow bell peppers
⅓ cup chopped scallions
½ cup diced zucchini
2 tablespoons lime juice
2 tablespoons olive oil
¼ cup minced fresh dill

Pour the boiling water over the couscous in a large bowl, cover, and let the couscous set for 15 minutes. Fluff the couscous with a fork, then let it cool to room temperature.

Meanwhile, slice the tops off the whole peppers. Core, seed, wash, and drain the peppers. If necessary, slice a little off the bottoms of the peppers so they will sit on a plate without falling over.

Combine the diced peppers, scallions, zucchini, and cooled couscous in a large mixing bowl. In a small bowl, combine the lime juice, olive oil, and dill, and mix well. Pour this dressing over the couscous mixture, and toss to coat.

Spoon one-sixth of the couscous mixture into each cored pepper. Cover the peppers with plastic wrap, and chill at least 1 hour.

Per serving: Calories 111, Protein 2 g, Fat 5 g, Carbohydrates 15 g, Calcium 11 mg, Fiber 3 g, Sodium 5 mg

SZECHUAN NOODLES

Devised by cookbook author Bryanna Clark Grogan who says: "I've been making some version of this recipe for about 20 years. It started out with a lot of oil and a hefty portion of chopped peanuts. I substituted a slightly thickened broth for the oil, cut the amount of peanuts in half, and added some greens. It's ready in the time it takes to boil the pasta!"

Yield: 5 servings (or 3 servings for teenage boys!)

Cook the pasta according to the directions on the package. Heat a large, lightly oiled or nonstick wok or skillet. Add and steam-fry the green onions and garlic for about 2 minutes. Mix the water, broth powder, cornstarch, soy sauce, ketchup, vinegar, chili paste, and sugar. Add this to the pan, and stir until it boils.

Add the vegetarian "ham," peanuts, cucumber, and spinach. Stir quickly over high heat until everything is hot. Drain the pasta and add to the wok or skillet. Toss quickly and serve immediately.

* If you have no Chinese or Szechuan chili paste, or have a soy allergy, try Thai or Vietnamese chili paste (check for fish sauce), or even Louisiana hot sauce, but the amount may differ.

**To thaw frozen spinach quickly, cook on HIGH in the microwave right in the box for 5 minutes, unwrap, and/or thaw under hot running water in a colander.

NOTE: To reheat leftovers, add a little water or broth, as the pasta soaks up the oil-free sauce when it cools.

1 lb. spaghettini
4 green onions, chopped
3 cloves garlic, minced
½ cup cold water
1 teaspoon low-sodium vegetarian broth powder
1 teaspoon cornstarch
⅓ cup soy sauce
2 tablespoons ketchup
1 tablespoon vinegar
1 tablespoon Szechuan hot bean paste (Chinese chili bean paste)*
1 teaspoon sugar or other sweetener
¼ cup chopped vegetarian "bacon" or "ham," or 2 tablespoons soy bacon chips or bits, soaked in 2 tablespoons boiling water
¼ cup chopped, dry-roasted peanuts
⅔ cup chopped, peeled cucumber, zucchini, or celery
1 (10-oz.) pkg. frozen chopped spinach, thawed and squeezed dry**

Per serving: Calories 144, Protein 7 g, Fat 4 g, Carbohydrates 19 g, Calcium 111 mg, Fiber 4 g, Sodium 1200 mg

TASTE OF MOROCCO

Hearty enough to feed a tribe of hungry Bedouins—or teeny boppers. Using frozen peppers cuts the cooking time to about 20 minutes.

1 zucchini, cubed
1 sweet potato or small winter squash, cubed
1 clove garlic, minced or pressed
1 tablespoon oil
¼ cup water
1 (15-oz.) can chick-peas
1 teaspoon ground cumin
½ teaspoon each: allspice, ground ginger, turmeric, and paprika
¼ teaspoon each: salt, cayenne, and cinnamon
1 red bell pepper, diced
1 yellow bell pepper, diced
2 cups uncooked couscous
½ cup raisins

Sauté the zucchini, sweet potato or squash, and garlic in the oil until partially cooked, about 5 minutes. Use water as necessary to keep the vegetables from sticking. Drain and rinse the chick-peas. Add the spices, chick-peas, and peppers to the pan. Cover and cook for about 5 minutes.

Meanwhile, place the couscous and raisins in another saucepan. Add enough water so that the couscous is covered by about ½ inch. Bring the mixture to a boil, then cover tightly, remove from the heat, and let set at least 10 minutes. Remove the cover from the pepper/chick-pea mixture, stir, and cook a few minutes longer to heat thoroughly and thicken. Serve the bean-pepper stew over the couscous.

Per serving: Calories 497, Protein 16 g, Fat 6 g, Carbohydrates 95 g, Calcium 74 mg, Fiber 16 g, Sodium 160 mg

TOFU FOO YUNG

This egg-cellent dish has all the flavor but none of the cholesterol of the Oriental favorite.

In a skillet or wok, sauté the snow peas, mushrooms, onions, and water chestnuts in the oil over low heat for about 5 minutes. When the vegetables are crisp-tender, mix in the bean sprouts. Remove from the heat and set aside.

Preheat the oven to 325°F.

Blend the 1¾ pounds tofu and the soy sauce until smooth and creamy. Pour into a bowl and mix in the ½ cup tofu, flour, nutritional yeast, and baking powder.

Mix the vegetables and tofu together well. On an oiled cookie sheet, make six to eight 5-inch rounds about ½ inch thick, using about ½ cup of the mixture for each round. Leave about 1 inch of space between the rounds. Bake for 30 minutes, flip over, and bake 15 more minutes. Serve hot over rice or noodles with Mushroom Gravy.

1 cup snow peas
1 cup sliced fresh mushrooms
8 green onions, cut into 1½-inch pieces
1 (8-oz) can water chestnuts, sliced
2 tablespoons oil
2 cups fresh bean sprouts
1¾ lbs. tofu, mashed
2 tablespoons soy sauce
½ cup mashed tofu
¾ cup unbleached white flour
3 tablespoons nutritional yeast (optional)
2 teaspoons baking powder

MUSHROOM GRAVY

Mix all the ingredients together in a saucepan. Cook over low heat, stirring until thickened.

2 cups cold water
4 tablespoons soy sauce
2 tablespoons cornstarch
½ cup finely diced fresh mushrooms

Per serving: Calories 297, Protein 16 g, Fat 10 g, Carbohydrates 32 g, Calcium 291 mg, Fiber 5 g, Sodium 1025 mg

TOFU NOT-A-TURKEY

Wondering what to replace the turkey with at holiday gatherings? Wonder no more! We'd say it's better than Mom's, but a PETA mom invented it—and it doesn't get any better than this!

Yield: 20 to 24 servings

6 lbs. firm tofu

Cornbread Stuffing:
1 cup diced onion
1 cup diced celery
1 tablespoon sesame oil
1 teaspoon parsley
½ teaspoon sage
½ teaspoon thyme
Salt and pepper, to taste
3 cups cubed whole wheat bread
2 cups cubed corn bread
½ cup vegetable broth
½ cup walnuts or pecans (optional)

Basting Liquid:
½ cup sesame oil
¼ cup soy sauce

One hour before cooking, mash the tofu and pack into a colander lined with cheesecloth or a clean towel. Place the colander over a large bowl to catch the liquid from the tofu. Weigh it down with a heavy object such as a can or a jar on top of a plate.

To make the stuffing, sauté the onion and celery in the sesame oil. Mix the seasonings into the cubed bread. Combine everything, adding enough vegetable broth to moisten. Add nuts if desired.

Preheat the oven to 400°F.

Press the tofu with your hands to form a hollow center, fill with the stuffing mixture, and press down. Flip the tofu onto an oiled baking sheet. Remove the towel or cheesecloth. Baste with the sesame oil and soy sauce mixture, cover with foil, and bake for 1 hour. Remove the foil, baste again, return to the hot oven, and bake ½ to 1 hour, or until golden. Transfer to a serving platter, and serve with gravy.

Sauté the onion in the oil until soft. Add the mushrooms and sauté for 1 minute more. Shake the flour and broth together in a jar, and add this to the onions and mushrooms. Mix in the soy sauce, and stir over low heat until thick.

Gravy:
1 onion, diced
2 tablespoons oil
1 cup sliced mushrooms
¼ cup flour
2 cups vegetable broth
½ cup soy sauce

Per serving: Calories 200, Protein 11 g, Fat 12 g, Carbohydrates 11 g, Calcium 145 mg, Fiber 2 g, Sodium 609 mg

VEGETARIAN FEIJOADA

This recipe makes enough to share, so throw a feijoada fiesta for all your friends. Don't forget to pass the hot sauce!

4 cups dried black (turtle) beans, soaked for at least 4 hours, rinsed, and drained
12 cups vegetarian broth
4 medium onions, chopped
1 (28-oz.) can diced tomatoes and juice
4 large cloves garlic, minced
2 teaspoons dried oregano
1 teaspoon liquid smoke
½ teaspoon cayenne pepper
4 cups long-grain brown rice
6 cups water
1 teaspoon salt
8 oranges, peeled and sliced ¼ inch thick (optional)
Greens (optional)
Onions, sliced and marinated in vinegar (optional)
Louisiana hot sauce, salsa, vinegar, or lemon juice (optional)

Place the soaked beans in a large pot with the broth, onions, tomatoes, garlic, oregano, liquid smoke, and cayenne. Bring to a boil, boil for several minutes, then reduce the heat, cover, and simmer for 2 to 3 hours, or until beans are tender. Add salt, to taste.

To pressure-cook, use a large, canning-sized pressure cooker, or do it in 2 batches in a 6-quart pressure cooker. Cook the bean ingredients at 15 lbs. pressure for 40 minutes.

About an hour before serving, heat a large, heavy saucepan with a tight lid. Add the dry rice and stir it over high heat with a wooden spoon for 2 minutes. Slowly add the water and then the salt. Bring to a boil, cover, and reduce the heat to low. Simmer for 45 minutes. Remove from the heat and let stand about 15 minutes before serving.

Use a large platter or tray to serve this dish. Drain the bean broth into a pitcher for serving on the side, mound the rice around the edge of the dish, and fill the center with the beans. Serve with greens, sliced, peeled oranges, sliced onions which have been marinated in vinegar for several hours, Louisiana hot sauce, and salsa, vinegar, or lemon juice.

Per serving: Calories 421, Protein 14 g, Fat 1 g, Carbohydrates 85 g, Calcium 126 mg, Fiber 13 g, Sodium 638 mg

ZUCCHINI BOATS

Ahoy, mateys! If this recipe doesn't tempt you to set sail on a culinary adventure, we'll walk the plank!

Yield: 3 servings

Slice the zucchini lengthwise and scoop out the pulp. Chop the pulp and set aside.

In a nonstick pan, brown the onion in the olive oil. Add the tofu or crumbled burger, chopped zucchini pulp, nutritional yeast, garlic salt, and oregano.

Pour the tomato sauce into a 9 x 11-inch pan. Place the zucchini "boats" in the sauce, and fill boats with the tofu mixture.

Cover with tin foil and bake for 30 minutes at 375°F. Remove the foil and bake 15 minutes more.

3 medium zucchini
1 medium onion, chopped
1 tablespoon olive oil
½ lb. tofu or vegetarian burger, crumbled
3 tablespoons nutritional yeast flakes
1 teaspoon garlic salt
½ teaspoon oregano
1 (16-oz.) jar tomato sauce (or homemade sauce—even better)

Per serving: Calories 227, Protein 12 g, Fat 8 g, Carbohydrates 26 g, Calcium 172 mg, Fiber 9 g, Sodium 1695 mg

CHARLOTTE-NOËLLE

"She's dead, I thought," said the PETA investigator. His heart went out to Charlotte-Noëlle at an auction of "downers"—sick, crippled, and injured animals—where he had been sent to take photographs. The 6-week-old piglet was lying on the ground, too weak from pneumonia to move, waiting to be auctioned off for dog food.

"But then," said our agent, "this little pink baby gave a tiny moan. I bought her immediately, slipped her inside my jacket and rushed her out of that place."

His first stop was at an animal sanctuary, where the employees bundled her in blankets and tucked her under heat lamps in a straw-filled barn stall. But the tiny piglet would only sleep when one of them stretched out next to her. Then she'd snuggle up as close as she could to whomever was nearest and bury her nose under the person's arm. The staff took turns sleeping next to her for many weeks.

Finally her body responded to love and nutrition. She began to recover and to follow the animal caretakers around like a big happy puppy, coming into the house at the sanctuary every day to sit politely and eat lunch with the employees.

When she was 4 months old, sanctuary employees took her to a farm owned by a vegetarian couple, who immediately fell in love with her playful personality and adopted her. She lives happily there today with two other rescued pigs, Sparky and Belle.

Her favorite foods are watermelon and the delicious tofu pumpkin pies her "stepmom" makes for her on winter holidays.

The minute Charlotte-Noëlle sees someone approach, she runs toward him or her as fast as her little legs will carry her, wiggling her ears and smiling, in love with life. Then she stands on her hind legs, front hooves against the fence, eyes sparkling, eager to be a friend.

SIDE DISHES

"The time will come when men such as I will look upon the murder of animals as they now look upon the murder of men."

—Leonardo da Vinci

LINGUINE WITH SMOKY TOMATO SAUCE

What makes this dish special is the chipotle pepper (actually a dried, smoked jalapeño) that imparts a hint of chocolate sweetness.

Yield: 2 to 3 servings

S I D E   D I S H E S

1-2 chipotle peppers
½ lb. linguine
2 medium shallots, diced
4 cloves garlic, minced
6 plum tomatoes, diced
Olive oil
Salt, to taste

Rehydrate the chipotle in enough water to cover it; let it set for 10 minutes. Once rehydrated, seed and dice it. Cook the pasta until it is al dente. Sauté the shallots, chipotle, and garlic for 3 minutes. Add tomatoes and simmer for 8 minutes more. After draining the pasta, lightly oil and salt it. Serve the smoky sauce over the linguine.

Per serving: Calories 196, Protein 6 g, Fat 0 g, Carbohydrates 41 g, Calcium 32 mg, Fiber 6 g, Sodium 55 mg

SAVORY NOODEL KUGEL

Classic kugel is held together with beaten eggs or soft cheese, but this *kinder* kugel is made with a creamy combination of blended tofu and savory spices.

Yield: 8 to 12 servings

Cook the pasta in lots of boiling, salted water until just tender, but not mushy. Drain in a colander. Preheat the oven to 350°F.

Blend the tofu, lemon juice, sugar, salt, and cayenne until very smooth in a food processor or in several batches in a blender. Combine the cooked, drained pasta, all but ½ cup of the blended tofu mixture, the onions, garlic, and Worcestershire sauce in a large bowl. Mix well and add salt, to taste. Place in a lightly oiled casserole or 9 x 13-inch baking pan, smoothing the top. Bake for ½ hour, or until golden and crusty on top. Spread the remaining tofu mixture on top, and serve hot. Sprinkle the top with soy Parmesan cheese before serving, if desired.

1 lb. fettuccine, broken in half
1½ lbs. firm or medium-firm tofu, crumbled
⅓ cup lemon juice
1½ teaspoons sugar or other sweetener
1 teaspoon salt
Dash of cayenne pepper
2 onions, minced
2 cloves garlic, minced or crushed
2 tablespoons Veggie Worcestershire Sauce, p. 25
Salt, to taste
Soy Parmesan for topping (optional)

Per serving: Calories 133, Protein 8 g, Fat 3 g, Carbohydrates 19 g, Calcium 86 mg, Fiber 1 g, Sodium 253 mg

CREAMY CHIVE MASHED POTATOES

The ultimate comfort food. Perfect with nut roasts, portobello mushrooms, or Tofu Not-a-Turkey, page 138.

Yield: 6 servings

5 large potatoes, peeled and boiled
1 cup liquid nondairy creamer
¼ cup chopped fresh chives
Salt, to taste

Place all the ingredients in a bowl, and whip until smooth.

Per serving: Calories 129, Protein 2 g, Fat 0 g, Carbohydrates 28 g,
Calcium 12 mg, Fiber 3 g, Sodium 12 mg

FRENCH-FRIED ONION STRING BEANS

An old-fashioned favorite—made even yummier without the ham or chicken broth.

Yield: 4 to 6 servings

2 (14.5-oz.) cans low-sodium
  French-style green beans, drained
1 (2.8-oz) can French-fried onions
3 tablespoons nutritional yeast
1 tablespoon vegetarian chicken-
  style broth powder
1 teaspoon garlic salt

Combine all the ingredients in a saucepan, and stir over medium heat until well-blended and hot.

Per serving: Calories 176, Protein 5 g, Fat 8 g, Carbohydrates 20 g,
Calcium 63 mg, Fiber 4 g, Sodium 667 mg

S
I
D
E

D
I
S
H
E
S

GARLIC STUFFED POTATOES

Good golly, these garlicky potatoes are good eatin'!

Bake the potatoes at 400°F for 1 hour. Allow to cool slightly.

Sauté the garlic in the olive oil over medium heat. Set aside.

Split open the tops of the potatoes, scoop out the pulp, and place in a bowl. Add the olive oil mixture to the bowl with salt and pepper, and whip with the potatoes. Fill the potato shells with the whipped potatoes. Sprinkle with paprika. Place on a tray and brown under the broiler for 10 minutes. Serve piping hot.

4 large baking potatoes
2 tablespoons olive oil
1 teaspoon chopped fresh garlic
Salt and pepper, to taste
Paprika

SIDE DISHES

Per serving: Calories 390, Protein 5 g, Fat 11 g, Carbohydrates 77 g, Calcium 30 mg, Fiber 8 g, Sodium 24 mg

POPEYE'S DELIGHT

This hearty, delicious dish will have you ready to sail the seven seas!

Yield: 6 to 8 servings

8 medium potatoes, peeled and
  diced
1 tablespoon olive oil
1 large onion, diced
3 cups chopped spinach, stems
  removed and tightly packed
½ teaspoon black pepper
1 teaspoon salt
4 cloves garlic, minced
1 cup soymilk
Salt, to taste

Place the potatoes in a large saucepan, and cover with water. Simmer over medium heat for 25 minutes, or until tender. Heat the oil in a skillet. Add the onions, spinach, pepper, and salt, and sauté for about 5 minutes. Add the garlic 1 minute before removing the spinach mixture from the heat. Drain the potatoes and mash. Add the spinach mixture, soymilk, and salt to taste. Mix well and serve.

Per serving: Calories 177, Protein 3 g, Fat 3 g, Carbohydrates 34 g,
Calcium 41 mg, Fiber 5 g, Sodium 335 mg

ROASTED ROSEMARY POTATOES

Calorie-counters often have to count roasted potatoes out, but the lemony marinade used here seasons these potatoes perfectly without a drop of oil.

Yield: 8 to 10 servings

Preheat the oven to 400°F.

In a large bowl, coat the potatoes with about 2½ cups of the marinade, and sprinkle with the rosemary and salt to taste. Spread the potatoes on 4 large, lightly oiled, dark-colored cookie sheets. (The dark color will help the potatoes brown.)

Bake on both racks of a 30-inch oven, if you have one, switching the pans from top to bottom halfway through. (If you only have a small oven, bake two pans at a time, then combine them all into two pans, and warm them in the oven before serving.) Bake the potatoes for about 1 hour, turning several times with a spatula, until they are golden brown and crispy. Add the last bit of marinade if the potatoes are getting dry. Serve hot.

6 lbs. well-scrubbed potatoes, either whole, tiny ones or larger ones (about 16 medium potatoes), cut into large cubes
1 recipe Marvelous Marinade, p. 152
⅓ cup fresh rosemary, chopped, or 2½-3 tablespoons dried rosemary
Salt, to taste

S I D E D I S H E S

Per serving: Calories 274, Protein 3 g, Fat 0 g, Carbohydrates 64 g, Calcium 17 mg, Fiber 6 g, Sodium 1022 mg

REALLY EASY RISOTTO

Does endlessly stirring traditional risotto make you stir crazy? Relax: This really good risotto is also really easy!

2 large onions, thinly sliced
2 cloves garlic, minced
1⅓ cups arborio or short grain rice
2½ cups vegetarian broth
⅔ cup dry white wine or non-alcoholic white wine
1 teaspoon dried rosemary
½ teaspoon salt
White pepper, to taste
¼-½ cup soy Parmesan (optional)

In a lightly oiled, heavy pot, steam-fry the onion until soft and nicely browned. Add the garlic toward the end of the cooking time. Add the remaining ingredients, except the pepper and soy Parmesan, and bring to a boil. Reduce the heat to low, and simmer, uncovered, until thick and creamy, stirring now and then for about 30 minutes. If there's not enough liquid at the end, add a tiny bit of water at a time. Add white pepper to taste and soy Parmesan, if desired.

Per serving: Calories 248, Protein 5 g, Fat 0 g, Carbohydrates 48 g, Calcium 38 mg, Fiber 3 g, Sodium 188 mg

POLENTA AND TOMATO STUFFED PEPPERS

Peter Piper would love to pick a peck of these polenta peppers—and so will you!

Yield: 4 to 6 servings

Preheat the oven to 375°F. Cut the tops off the peppers, and scoop out the insides. Place on a cookie sheet.

Sauté the garlic in the olive oil over medium heat. Add the tomatoes, salt, and pepper. Heat briefly and stir into the polenta.

Fill the peppers with the polenta mixture, and sprinkle with paprika. Cook for 30 to 40 minutes.

1 green, 1 red, 1 yellow, and
  1 orange bell pepper
½ teaspoon minced fresh garlic
1 tablespoon olive oil
2 medium tomatoes, diced
1 teaspoon salt
½ teaspoon pepper
1 (1-lb.) pkg. cooked polenta
Paprika

Per serving: Calories 212, Protein 4 g, Fat 3 g, Carbohydrates 40 g,
Calcium 12 mg, Fiber 5 g, Sodium 432 mg

POLENTA WITH ZUCCHINI AND TOMATOES

If you think polenta has potential, then pop this in a pan and partake!

Yield: 4 to 6 servings

In a nonstick pan, sauté the garlic in the olive oil, if desired, or heat with the tomato sauce, tomato, salt, and zucchini over medium heat. Stir regularly until the zucchini starts to soften. Add the polenta and cook several minutes more until hot.

1 teaspoon fresh minced garlic
1 tablespoon olive oil (optional)
¼-½ cup tomato or spaghetti sauce
1 medium tomato, chopped
1 teaspoon salt
2 medium zucchini, thinly sliced
1 (1-lb.) pkg. cooked polenta, cut
  into bite-sized pieces

Per serving: Calories 186, Protein 5 g, Fat 0 g, Carbohydrates 40 g,
Calcium 22 mg, Fiber 5 g, Sodium 542 mg

GLAZED ROOT VEGETABLES

A wonderful way to enjoy winter veggies, this recipe is sure to become a favorite at all your holiday get-togethers.

Yield: 8 servings

2 large carrots, scrubbed or peeled
2 parsnips, peeled
2 medium turnips, peeled
1 rutabaga, peeled
2 large yellow onions, peeled
1 cup Marvelous Marinade (see below)
¼ cup maple syrup or fruit concentrate syrup

Preheat the oven to 400°F. Cut the vegetables into even-sized wedges (about ½ inch thick and 3 inches long). Toss them with the marinade and maple syrup or fruit concentrate syrup, and spread on 2 lightly oiled, shallow baking pans. Bake for 45 to 60 minutes, turning occasionally, until the vegetables are tender and glazed. Serve hot.

Per serving: Calories 115, Protein 1 g, Fat 0 g, Carbohydrates 26 g, Calcium 64 mg, Fiber 4 g, Sodium 382 mg

MARVELOUS MARINADE

2 cups cold water
2 tablespoons cornstarch
2 tablespoons chicken-style vegetarian broth, or 2 vegetarian broth cubes
¾ cup lemon juice
Grated zest of 1 lemon
2 tablespoons herbal salt
4 large cloves garlic, crushed
1 teaspoon dried oregano or other herb of choice, or 1 tablespoon fresh herbs

In a heavy saucepan, mix the cold water, cornstarch, and vegetable broth. Cook, stirring constantly, over high heat until the mixture has thickened and come to a boil. Add the remaining ingredients.

For a sweeter glaze, add 2 tablespoons of maple syrup to each ½ cup of marinade.

Makes 3 cups.

GREEN BEAN STROGANOFF

If your family won't normally touch green beans with a 10-foot fork, keep reading! The creamy sauce transforms any veggie from dull to delicious.

Yield: 6 servings

Heat a large, heavy, nonstick or lightly oiled skillet, over high heat. Add the onions and garlic, and steam-fry with 3 tablespoons of the wine until the onion starts to soften (using a little water if necessary). Add the green beans, mushrooms, basil, and remaining wine. Cover and cook over medium heat for 5 minutes, or until the beans are done to your liking.

Meanwhile, mix the tofu, water, soy sauce, lemon juice, and sugar in a blender or food processor until very smooth. Pour this into the pan with the vegetables. Turn the heat to low, and heat the mixture gently. Add salt and pepper, to taste. Serve hot over hot, cooked linguine or fettuccine noodles.

3 large onions, thinly sliced
2 cloves garlic, minced
⅓ cup dry white wine
1½ lbs. frozen or fresh, whole, small green beans
¾ lb. fresh mushrooms, sliced
1 tablespoon dried basil, or 3 tablespoons chopped fresh
1 (12.3-oz). pkg. firm silken tofu (1½ cups)
6 tablespoons water
⅓ cup soy sauce or tamari
3 tablespoons lemon juice
¼ teaspoon sugar or other sweetener
Salt and freshly ground black pepper, to taste

S I D E D I S H E S

Per serving: Calories 154, Protein 10 g, Fat 2 g, Carbohydrates 19 g, Calcium 133 mg, Fiber 5 g, Sodium 853 mg

SWEET-AND-SOUR VEGETABLES

This easy Thai stir-fry can be thrown together at the last minute if you have the vegetables prepared. It's hot!

Yield: 6 servings

1 tablespoon minced garlic
6 whole baby corn (canned is fine)
24 chunks canned pineapple
½ cucumber, peeled and cut into rounds
3 medium onions, halved and thinly sliced
3 medium-ripe, firm tomatoes, quartered
6 green onions, cut into 1-inch pieces
2 large red bell peppers, seeded and cut into thin strips
3 tablespoons light soy sauce
1 tablespoon sugar or other sweetener
1 teaspoon white pepper
1 teaspoon dried red chili flakes, or to taste
1 tablespoon cornstarch mixed with ¾ cup cold water

Lightly oil a large wok or skillet, and heat over high heat. Add the garlic and a few sprinkles of water; stir-fry for a few seconds until the water evaporates. Add each vegetable or fruit listed in turn, stirring constantly and adding just a bit of water, if needed, to keep from sticking. When the vegetables are crisp-tender, add the soy sauce, sugar, white pepper, chili, then the cornstarch mixture; stir until it has thickened. Turn onto a serving dish, and serve immediately with steamed rice.

Per serving: Calories 99, Protein 2 g, Fat 0 g, Carbohydrates 20 g,
Calcium 45 mg, Fiber 4 g, Sodium 312 mg

BAKED GOODS
&
SPREADS

"If you're violent to yourself by putting things into your body that violate its spirit, it will be difficult not to perpetuate that [violence] onto someone else."

—Dexter Scott King

CHALLAH

Traditional Jewish egg bread goes egg-free in this vegan version.

Yield: 2 loaves or 32 rolls

2 cups warm water
1 package baking yeast
¼ cup soymilk powder
1 tablespoon lemon juice
2 tablespoons salt
½ cup liquid sweetener
¼ cup sugar
1 cup leftover mashed potatoes
   (½ lb. russet potatoes, cooked and
   mashed), or 1 cup instant mashed
   potato flakes mixed with ⅔ cup
   boiling water
¼ teaspoon turmeric
½ cup wheat germ
5 cups unbleached flour

In a large mixing bowl, mix the warm water and yeast. When the yeast is dissolved, add all the other ingredients except the flour.

Mix in the flour and knead well for 5 to 10 minutes, using as little additional flour as possible. This dough should be soft and a bit sticky.

Place in a greased bowl, and let rise overnight in the refrigerator. (This dough handles best when cold.) If you wish, you can also let it rise until doubled either once or twice.

Preheat the oven to 350°F. Divide the risen dough equally in half. Make braided loaves. Just before baking, brush with Eggless "Egg" Wash (see below), and sprinkle with sesame or poppy seeds. Bake for 45 minutes.

You can also make 32 small rolls. Cover and rise until doubled. Bake at 350°F for 20 to 25 minutes for rolls.

Per roll: Calories 90, Protein 3 g, Fat 0 g, Carbohydrates 19 g, Calcium 31 mg, Fiber 1 g, Sodium 356 mg

Eggless "Egg" Wash: Use this in place of egg white to help toppings adhere to the tops of loaves or for a shiny crust. Mix ½ cup cold water with 1 teaspoon cornstarch in a small saucepan. Stir and cook over high heat until thickened and clear.

SUPER SOY BREAD

Making sandwiches with this nutty-tasting, high-protein bread gives new meaning to the term "power lunch."

Yield: 2 loaves or 16 buns

Scald the soymilk, dissolve the sweetener in it, and cool to lukewarm. Sprinkle the baking yeast over the top, and let stand until the yeast starts foaming.

Stir in the salt and white flour, and beat until smooth. Stir in the soy flour, and beat until smooth. Add the whole wheat flour, and knead until smooth. Cover and let rise until almost doubled in bulk.

Preheat the oven to 350°F.

Punch down the dough and form 2 loaves or 16 buns. Let rise again until almost doubled in bulk. Bake the loaves for about 45 minutes or the buns for about 20 minutes. Brush the tops with soy oil.

3 cups soymilk
2 tablespoons sweetener of your choice
1 tablespoon baking yeast
2 teaspoons salt
4 cups unbleached white flour
2 cups soy flour
3-4 cups whole wheat flour

Per bun: Calories 273, Protein 13 g, Fat 5 g, Carbohydrates 46 g, Calcium 83 mg, Fiber 6 g, Sodium 274 mg

Cows are gas guzzlers compared to energy-efficient soy! A quarter gallon of gasoline is needed to produce every pound of beef, but 40 pounds of soybeans could be produced with the same amount of fossil fuel.

BAKED GOODS & SPREADS

APPLE-MAPLE MUFFINS

For a real sweet treat, make a quick glaze for these muffins by combining 3 tablespoons powdered sugar with 1 tablespoon maple syrup.

BAKED GOODS & SPREADS

Yield: 12 muffins

1⅓ cups flour
1 cup rolled oats
½ cup sugar
1 tablespoon baking powder
1½ teaspoons ground cinnamon
½ cup soymilk
5⅓ tablespoons dairy-free margarine, melted
¼ cup maple syrup
¼ cup unsweetened applesauce
1 cup chopped apples
Pecan halves

Heat the oven to 400°F. Line 12 medium muffin cups with paper baking liners.

Combine the flour, rolled oats, sugar, baking powder, and cinnamon in a large bowl. In a medium bowl, combine the soymilk, margarine, maple syrup, and applesauce. Add the soymilk mixture to the dry ingredients, and stir until just moistened. Gently stir in the chopped apples.

Fill the muffin cups half full, and top each with a pecan half. Bake for 20 to 25 minutes, or until a toothpick inserted in the center comes out clean. Let cool on wire racks.

Per muffin: Calories 188, Protein 3 g, Fat 7 g, Carbohydrates 30 g, Calcium 96 mg, Fiber 2 g, Sodium 167 mg

COCOA-BANANA MUFFINS

The art of substitution is easy in baked goods. With mashed bananas, you don't need to add eggs.

Yield: 12 muffins

Preheat the oven to 400°F. Line 12 medium muffin cups with paper baking liners.

Combine the flour, oats, brown sugar, cocoa, baking powder, and baking soda in a large bowl. In a medium bowl, combine the mashed bananas, soymilk, margarine, and vanilla. Add the banana mixture to the dry ingredients, and stir until just moistened.

Spoon the batter into the prepared muffin cups, and bake for 20 to 25 minutes until a toothpick inserted into the center of the muffins comes out clean. Cool on a wire rack.

1¼ cups all-purpose flour
1 cup rolled oats
½ cup firmly packed brown sugar
⅓ cup unsweetened cocoa
1 tablespoon baking powder
¼ teaspoon baking soda
1 cup mashed bananas
  (about 3 small)
½ cup soymilk
5⅓ tablespoons margarine, melted
1 teaspoon vanilla

BAKED GOODS & SPREADS

Per muffin: Calories 168, Protein 4 g, Fat 5 g, Carbohydrates 25 g,
Calcium 96 mg, Fiber 3 g, Sodium 186 mg

DECIDEDLY DELICIOUS DANISH

If you rely on cheese Danish and a cup of joe for your a.m. get-up-and-go, you'll love this sweet homemade treat. But you better make lots, or you will wonder where they all went!

Yield: 24 Danish

Dough:
1 tablespoon active dry yeast
1 tablespoon sweetener of your
 choice
1 cup warm water
2 cups unbleached white flour
3 tablespoons sweetener of your
 choice
½ cup oil
¼ cup sweetener of your choice
1 teaspoon salt
About 1½ cups more unbleached
 white flour (2½ cups if you used
 a liquid sweetener)

Tofu Filling:
½ cup water
¼ cup oil
1 cup crumbled soft tofu
¼ cup fresh lemon juice
½ cup sweetener of your choice
½ teaspoon salt
2 tablespoons unbleached white
 flour

To make the dough, dissolve together the dry yeast, 1 tablespoon sweetener, and 1 cup warm water, and let stand 5 minutes. Mix in 2 cups white flour and 3 tablespoons sweetener, beat well, and let rise until doubled.

Dissolve together the ½ cup oil, ¼ cup sweetener, and 1 teaspoon salt, then mix into the flour and yeast mixture with your hands. Add the 1½ or 2½ cups white flour to make a kneadable dough. Knead until smooth and soft, but not sticky. Let rise until double again.

To make the tofu filling, combine the ½ cup water, ¼ cup oil, and 1 cup soft tofu in a blender until smooth and creamy. Pour into a saucepan, and whisk in the lemon juice, ½ cup sweetener, ½ teaspoon salt, and 2 tablespoons white flour. Cook over medium heat, stirring constantly until thickened. Remove from the heat and cool before filling the Danish dough.

Preheat the oven to 350°F. Roll the dough out to ⅛ inch thick. Brush with oil and cut into 4 x 4-inch squares. Place 1 scant tablespoon of filling in the center of each square. You can add about 1 scant tablespoon of cherry or blueberry pie filling on the top of the tofu filling. Fold 2 of the opposite corners of the dough toward the middle and pinch together. Take the remaining unfolded corners, and curl them in toward the filling. Let rise 5 minutes. Place on a well-oiled cookie sheet. Leave ½ to 1 inch of space between each Danish. Bake for about 15 minutes or until light golden brown. Brush with oil for the last 3 minutes of baking.

Prune Danish: Make a prune filling by placing 1 lb. pitted prunes and 2 cups water in a saucepan, cover, and cook until tender. Purée in a food processor, and stir in 1½ tablespoons lemon juice. To assemble the Danish, place 1 scant tablespoon of the prune filling in the center of each square instead of the tofu filling. Bring all four corners toward the middle, and pinch together. Place on a well-oiled cookie sheet, and follow the baking instructions for Tofu Danish.

Per Danish (with tofu filling): Calories 161, Protein 3 g, Fat 7 g, Carbohydrates 21 g, Calcium 47 mg, Fiber 1 g, Sodium 135 mg
Per Danish (with prune filling): Calories 165, Protein 2 g, Fat 5 g, Carbohydrates 29 g, Calcium 39 mg, Fiber 1 g, Sodium 90 mg

INCREDIBLE CORN BREAD

The perfect accompaniment to veggie chili and other Southwestern fare.

Yield: 9 pieces

Preheat the oven to 350°F. Combine the dry ingredients. Add the oil and soymilk, and mix well. Pour into a lightly oiled 8 x 8-inch pan, and bake for 30 minutes.

1 cup cornmeal
1 cup flour
2 teaspoons baking powder
2 teaspoons sugar
1 teaspoon salt
2 tablespoons oil
1½ cups soymilk

Per piece: Calories 301, Protein 4 g, Fat 3 g, Carbohydrates 62 g, Calcium 80 mg, Fiber 2 g, Sodium 337 mg

LEMON POPPY SEED BREAD

A delicious and versatile bread—great for Sunday brunch or afternoon tea. It also makes an elegant dessert!

Yield: 16 slices

Bread:
⅓ cup dairy-free margarine
1 cup sugar
Egg replacer, equivalent to 2 eggs
1½ cups sifted all-purpose flour
1½ teaspoons baking powder
¼ teaspoon salt
½ cup soymilk
Grated rind of 1 lemon
1 (12½-oz.) can poppy seed filling

Glaze:
¼ cup sugar
Juice of ½ lemon

Preheat the oven to 350°F. Lightly oil a loaf pan, and set aside. Cream the margarine and gradually add the 1 cup sugar, beating well. Add ½ of the egg replacer, and beat well. Add the remaining egg replacer, and beat well again. Combine the flour, baking powder, and salt, and add to the creamed mixture alternately with the soymilk. Mix well after each addition. Stir in the lemon rind and poppy seed filling. Pour the batter into the loaf pan.

Bake for 50 minutes or until a toothpick inserted in the center comes out clean.

Combine the ¼ cup sugar and lemon juice, and stir well. Spoon over the bread immediately after removing it from the oven, while it is still in the pan. Cool in the pan for 10 minutes; remove from the pan and cool completely on a wire rack.

Per slice: Calories 240, Protein 5 g, Fat 10 g, Carbohydrates 30 g, Calcium 307 mg, Fiber 0 g, Sodium 132 mg

PIÑA COLADA BREAD

PETA's education manager, Bobbi Hoffman, whips up this tropical delight for bake sale fund-raisers—and it always sells out!

Yield: 20 to 24 slices

Preheat the oven to 350°F. Oil and flour 2 loaf pans, and set aside. Combine the flour, baking soda, and salt, and set aside. Combine the oil, egg replacer, sugar, and extracts in a large bowl with an electric mixer. Mix well. Gradually add the dry ingredients to the creamed mixture, stirring until all the ingredients are moistened. Stir in the pineapple and coconut. Spoon the mixture into the loaf pans.

Bake for 55 minutes or until a wooden toothpick inserted in the center comes out clean (check after 45 minutes). Cool in the pans for 10 minutes. Remove to a wire rack, and cool completely.

*To reduce the fat, you can substitute ¼ cup applesauce for ¼ cup of the vegetable oil.

3 cups all-purpose flour
1 teaspoon baking soda
1 teaspoon salt
1¼ cups vegetable oil*
Egg replacer, equivalent to 3 eggs
1½ cups sugar
1 teaspoon pineapple extract
1 teaspoon rum extract
2 cups drained, crushed pineapple
1 cup shredded, sweetened coconut

BAKED GOODS & SPREADS

Per slice: Calories 301, Protein 3 g, Fat 19 g, Carbohydrates 29 g, Calcium 49 mg, Fiber 10 g, Sodium 131 mg

VERY BLUEBERRY MUFFINS

These mouth-watering muffins will make any brunch "berry" special.

Yield: 12 muffins

Dry Ingredients:
1¼ cups unbleached white or
    whole wheat pastry flour
⅓ cup oat flour
1 teaspoon baking powder
1 teaspoon baking soda
1 teaspoon salt
½-1 cup chopped dried fruit,
    or 1 cup chopped, well-drained
    fresh fruit or berries
½ teaspoon cinnamon
½ teaspoon nutmeg

½ lb. medium-firm tofu
¼-½ cup sugar
½ cup water or fruit juice (if you
    are adding very juicy fruit, use
    only ⅓ cup)
1 tablespoon lemon juice
1-2 tablespoons nutritional yeast
    flakes (optional)
1 tablespoon molasses (optional)
1-3 tablespoons vanilla or other
    flavor extract or grated citrus zest
1 cup fresh or well-drained,
    thawed frozen blueberries

Preheat the oven to 350°F. In a medium bowl, mix together the dry ingredients.

In a blender, mix the tofu, sugar, water, lemon juice, yeast flakes, molasses, and vanilla until very smooth. If you prefer not to use sugar, replace the sugar, water, and lemon juice with 1 (6-oz.) can thawed, frozen apple juice concentrate (¾ cup) plus 1 tablespoon water. You can omit this extra water if you are adding very juicy fruit.

Mix the blueberries with 2 tablespoons of the flour mixture.

Pour the blended mixture into the flour mixture, and stir just until all of the dry ingredients are well moistened. Fold the blueberries into the batter. Spoon the batter evenly into 12 lightly oiled or nonstick muffin cups. Bake for 20 minutes. If the muffins are too crusty for your taste, loosen them and turn them on their sides in the pan, then cover with a clean tea towel for 5 minutes while still hot from the oven.

Serve with jam. These freeze and reheat well.

Per muffin: Calories 131, Protein 3 g, Fat 1 g, Carbohydrates 27 g,
Calcium 69 mg, Fiber 1 g, Sodium 286 mg

BETTER BREAD SPREAD

Keep a tub on hand in the fridge. Use it on sandwiches, toast, veggies—you'll never go back to plain margarine!

Yield: ¾ cup

Bring the margarine to room temperature or soften with a spoon. Combine with the remaining ingredients, and store in the refrigerator.

½ cup dairy-free margarine
¼ cup chives
2 teaspoons garlic powder
Salt, to taste

Per tablespoon: Calories 68, Protein 0 g, Fat 6 g, Carbohydrates 0 g, Calcium 3 mg, Fiber 0 g, Sodium 89 mg

NUTTIN' BUTTER SPREAD

Nothing is better than graham crackers or toasted bagels topped with this sweet spread. Keep some in the fridge for quick snacks.

Yield: 1 cup

Combine the peanut butter, maple syrup, orange juice, cinnamon, and allspice, and stir until smooth. Stir in the dried fruits, and store in the refrigerator.

6 tablespoons peanut butter
4 tablespoons maple syrup
4 tablespoons orange juice
¾ teaspoon cinnamon
¼ teaspoon allspice
1 tablespoon raisins
1 tablespoon chopped dried figs, dates, or other dried fruit

Per tablespoon: Calories 53, Protein 2 g, Fat 2 g, Carbohydrates 6 g, Calcium 8 mg, Fiber 1 g, Sodium 3 mg

ROASTED PEPPER "CREAM CHEESE"

This wonderful red pepper spread will give your bagels a boost! It's great for a mid-morning snack or a light lunch.

Yield: 4 servings

BAKED GOODS & SPREADS

½ lb. soft tofu, well-drained
1 tablespoon soymilk
1 tablespoon rice wine vinegar
1 teaspoon brown rice syrup
⅛ teaspoon ground white pepper
¼ to ⅓ cup chopped roasted red bell peppers
2 scallions, minced
1 tablespoon pickle relish

Crumble the tofu into a blender or food processor. Add the soymilk, vinegar, brown rice syrup, and white pepper, and process until smooth.

Place the tofu mixture in a small bowl, and stir in the red bell peppers, scallions, and pickle relish. Cover and refrigerate until chilled, at least 1 hour.

TOP TIP: This recipe is very versatile. Instead of adding red peppers, scallions, and pickle relish to the tofu base, try your favorite combination of veggies, such as chopped sun-dried tomatoes and Kalamata olives with a dash of oregano, or grated carrots, walnuts, and raisins (leave out the white pepper for this one). Add a little water and you have a delectable dip!

Per serving: Calories 58, Protein 4 g, Fat 2 g, Carbohydrates 4 g, Calcium 65 mg, Fiber 1 g, Sodium 32 mg

DESSERTS

"The modern laying hen is the most miserable of birds."

—Lord Houghton

AWESOME APPLE CAKE

An easy way to eat an apple a day. Great served as is or try drizzling with glaze, dolloping with nondairy whipped topping, or swathing in vanilla frosting.

Yield: 16 servings

1¼ cups vegetable oil
2 cups sugar
Egg replacer, equivalent to 2 eggs
3 teaspoons vanilla
3 cups sifted flour
1½ teaspoons baking soda
1 teaspoon salt
1 cup chopped pecans
3 cups diced apples

Preheat the oven to 350°F. Combine the oil, sugar, egg replacer, and vanilla, and stir well. Add the sifted flour, baking soda, and salt, beat by hand, then add the pecans and apples. Pour into a 10-inch bundt pan, and bake for 1 hour and 15 minutes.

Per serving: Calories 388, Protein 4 g, Fat 21 g, Carbohydrates 45 g, Calcium 48 mg, Fiber 2 g, Sodium 221 mg

"CREAM"-FILLED ORANGE CRUMB CAKE

This irresistible orange cake would be a special treat at a sophisticated birthday party. But it's so delicious, you might just find yourself celebrating "un-birthdays" too!

Yield: 16 servings

Preheat the oven to 350°F.

For the first layer, combine the flour, sweetener, oil, orange zest, and salt in a food processor until blended. Add the walnuts and process until chopped. Press the mixture into the bottom and up the sides of a bundt pan.

For the second layer, blend the ingredients for the second layer together in a food processor or blender until smooth and creamy. Pour and spread on top of the first layer.

For the third layer, mix together the flour, walnuts, baking powder, baking soda, cinnamon, salt, and nutmeg. Beat together the soymilk, sweetener, oil, and orange juice, add the dry ingredients, and beat until smooth. Pour and spread this mixture over the second layer, being careful not to stir the second and third layers together. Bake for 40 to 45 minutes. Let cool 15 minutes, then loosen the edges, and turn out onto a rack to cool.

First Layer:
1 cup unbleached flour
½ cup granulated sweetener of your choice
2 tablespoons oil
1½ tablespoons organic orange zest
½ teaspoon salt
½ cup chopped walnuts

Second Layer:
1 lb. tofu
½ cup granulated sweetener of your choice
2 tablespoons cornstarch
1 tablespoon vanilla
½ teaspoon salt

Third Layer:
2 cups unbleached flour
½ cup chopped walnuts
2 teaspoons baking powder
½ teaspoon baking soda
½ teaspoon cinnamon
½ teaspoon salt
⅛ teaspoon nutmeg
1½ cups soymilk
1 cup granulated sweetener of your choice
2 tablespoons oil
4 tablespoons orange juice

Per serving: Calories 247, Protein 4 g, Fat 9 g, Carbohydrates 29 g, Calcium 18 mg, Fiber 4 g, Sodium 91 mg

D
E
S
S
E
R
T
S

169

PUMPKIN SPICE CAKE

You'll find yourself dreaming of this heavenly treat days after it's gone.

Yield: 9 servings

DESSERTS

Cake:
1⅔ cups flour
1 cup packed brown sugar
1 teaspoon allspice
1 teaspoon baking soda
½ teaspoon salt
½ cup water
⅓ cup vegetable oil
1 teaspoon vinegar
½ cup canned pumpkin
Powdered sugar

Frosting:
⅓ cup thawed apple juice
  concentrate
⅓ cup maple syrup
½ teaspoon cider vinegar
Grated zest of one orange
1 tablespoon cornstarch
1 tablespoon water
1¾ cups crumbled firm silken tofu

Heat the oven to 350°F. Mix the flour, brown sugar, allspice, baking soda, and salt in an unoiled 8 x 8 x 2-inch baking pan. Stir in the remaining ingredients, and bake for 35 to 40 minutes, until cooked through. Allow to cool on a wire rack before frosting.

Mix the apple juice concentrate, maple syrup, cider vinegar, and orange zest in a small saucepan, and bring to a boil. Let simmer for 5 minutes. Mix together the cornstarch and water, and stir into the saucepan. Simmer until the mixture thickens, stirring continuously. Blend this syrup and the tofu in a food processor until smooth. Frost the cooled cake.

Per serving: Calories 290, Protein 6 g, Fat 9 g, Carbohydrates 45 g,
Calcium 84 mg, Fiber 2 g, Sodium 238 mg

ALMOND TARTS

These little confections look like they jumped right out of a Beatrix Potter book. And they taste even better than they look!

Yield: 30 tarts

To make the pastry, place all the ingredients in a food processor, and process just enough to form a ball. Do not overprocess. Transfer the dough to a sheet of waxed paper, flatten into a circle, and refrigerate for 1 hour.

To make the almond filling, beat the almonds with the shortening and the sugar. Add the crushed vanilla wafers and the vanilla extract. Add enough soymilk to make a soft mixture.

To assemble the tarts, roll out the dough and cut circles the size of the bottom of muffin tins; line the bottom of the muffin tins with the pastry. Put a small dab of jam in the center. Cover with the almond mixture, and bake at 450°F for 12-15 minutes.

Pastry:
9 tablespoons vegetable shortening
4 tablespoons water
Pinch of salt
2 cups all-purpose flour

Almond filling:
½ lb. ground almonds
1 cup dairy-free, butter-flavored vegetable shortening
1 cup sugar
1 cup crushed vanilla wafers or cupcake crumbs
A few drops of vanilla extract
A small amount of soymilk
Your favorite jam

Per tart: Calories 206, Protein 2 g, Fat 13 g, Carbohydrates 19 g, Calcium 38 mg, Fiber 1 g, Sodium 125 mg

DESSERTS

BERRY MEDLEY PIE

Get a little carried away on your last berry-picking trip? This yummy, crumbly delight is the perfect cure for "berry overload."

Crust:
8 tablespoons flour
1 tablespoon sugar
1 teaspoon baking powder
4 tablespoons dairy-free margarine, softened
3-4 tablespoons rice milk

Filling:
3-4 cups fresh or frozen berries (blueberries, raspberries, and strawberries work well)
1 tablespoon sugar
2 tablespoons instant tapioca, ground to a powder in your blender

Topping:
4 tablespoons flour
6 tablespoons vanilla-flavored or plain sugar
4 tablespoons dairy-free margarine, softened

Combine the flour, sugar, and baking powder. Add the margarine and blend with a pastry blender or a fork. Add the rice milk (use more if needed to get the dough to hold together). Form it into a ball, spread evenly into an oiled pie dish, and set aside.

Place the berries in a mixing bowl, and sprinkle with the sugar and tapioca. Toss until the berries are coated. Fill the pie crust with the berries.

Preheat the oven to 325°F. Combine the flour and sugar. Add the margarine and mix with your finger tips, forming crumbs. Continue mixing until everything is combined. Crumble the topping evenly over the pie, and bake for approximately 1 hour.

Per serving: Calories 232, Protein 1 g, Fat 12 g, Carbohydrates 30 g, Calcium 57 mg, Fiber 2 g, Sodium 193 mg

THE BEST APPLE STREUSEL PIE

A slice of heaven on a plate—one bite will have your taste buds singing like a choir of angels!

Yield: 8 servings

Preheat the oven to 350°F.

Peel and slice the apples, and place in a large bowl. In a small bowl, mix ½ cup of the sugar and the cinnamon. Add to the apples until they are coated, then put the apples in the pie crust. Mix the remaining ½ cup sugar, the flour, and margarine until crumbly. Add small amounts of flour if necessary until small crumbs form. Sprinkle the crumbs over the pie, covering completely.

Bake 40 minutes until slightly browned.

8 baking or "pie" apples (a mixture of Granny Smith and MacIntosh works well)
1 cup sugar
1 teaspoon cinnamon
1 deep-dish vegan pie crust
¾ cup flour
½ cup dairy-free margarine

**D
E
S
S
E
R
T
S**

Per serving: Calories 331, Protein 3 g, Fat 18 g, Carbohydrates 38 g, Calcium 59 mg, Fiber 5 g, Sodium 275 mg

Animals raised for food in the United States eat one-third of the world's total grain harvest.

BLUEBERRY "CHEESE" CAKE

If you thought the hardest thing about giving up cheese was no more cheesecake, this recipe is for you. It's deceptively simple and decidedly delicious. It's also terrific topped with cherries, strawberries, or tofu "sour cream."

Yield: 8 servings

2 (8-oz.) containers plain nondairy cream cheese
1 cup sugar
Juice from one whole lemon
Dash of vanilla
Graham cracker crust
2 cups fresh or frozen (unthawed) blueberries
⅓ cup thawed apple juice concentrate
2 tablespoons cornstarch

Mix or blend together the nondairy cream cheese, sugar, lemon juice, and vanilla, and pour into the graham cracker crust. Bake at 350°F for 60 minutes, or until the top is golden brown. Allow to cool.

Mix together the blueberries, apple juice concentrate, and cornstarch in a medium saucepan. Cook over medium heat until the mixture thickens, stirring frequently but gently in order to keep the berries whole. Spread the topping over the cheesecake.

Per serving: Calories 358, Protein 3 g, Fat 14 g, Carbohydrates 55 g, Calcium 13 mg, Fiber 1 g, Sodium 243 mg

BOBBI'S BLISSFUL CHOCOLATE-RUM PIE

Chocoholics, take note: This creamy pie is addictive! (And it'll even tempt "tofu-haters.")

Line a 9-inch pie plate with foil. Stir together the margarine, baking chocolate, and 2 cups coconut. Press the coconut mixture into the bottom and sides of the pie plate. Chill until firm, at least 1 hour. Remove the coconut crust from the pie plate, carefully peel off the foil, then return to the pie plate.

In a blender, purée the tofu until smooth. Add the chocolate chips, sugar, and rum extract, and continue to blend until smooth. Pour the tofu mixture into the coconut crust, and chill for at least 2 hours.

Before serving, garnish the pie with a little toasted coconut, if desired.

2 tablespoons dairy-free margarine, melted
4 oz. (4 squares) semi-sweet baking chocolate, melted
2 cups flaked coconut
2 (12.3-oz.) pkgs. firm silken tofu (3 cups)
2 cups semi-sweet chocolate chips, melted
½ cup confectioners' sugar
1½ teaspoons rum extract
Toasted flaked coconut for garnish (optional)

Per serving: Calories 385, Protein 7 g, Fat 29 g, Carbohydrates 24 g, Calcium 31 mg, Fiber 5 g, Sodium 46 mg

EASY PUMPKIN PIE

Don't tell your relatives that tofu replaces the eggs and cream in this pumpkin pie until after they tell you it's the best they ever tasted.

Yield: 8 servings

1 lb. silken tofu
1 (16-oz.) can solid pack pumpkin
¾ cup granulated sugar
1 teaspoon cinnamon
1 teaspoon vanilla
½ teaspoon ginger
½ teaspoon nutmeg
¼ teaspoon salt
¼ teaspoon ground cloves
¼ teaspoon allspice
Egg replacer, equivalent to 1 egg
1 (9-inch) pie crust

Preheat the oven to 375°F. Blend the tofu in a blender or food processor until creamy and smooth. Add the remaining ingredients except the pie crust, and blend well. Pour into the crust, and bake about 1 hour, or until a toothpick inserted in the center comes out almost clean.

Per serving: Calories 237, Protein 6 g, Fat 9 g, Carbohydrates 34 g, Calcium 60 mg, Fiber 3 g, Sodium 165 mg

EASY DESSERT SHORTCUTS

It's easier than you think to "veganize" your favorite dessert recipes. Recipes that call for pudding mixes can be made with vegan kosher pudding (available in the kosher sections of major supermarkets) and soymilk. Tofu "sour cream" and "cream cheese"—both commercial brands and those made from scratch—work great in most recipes. Check labels; lots of cake and brownie mixes are vegan. Even many ready-made frostings are vegan! When eggs are called for, they can be replaced with vegan ingredients (see egg replacers, p. 10).

KAREN'S CHOCOLATE-PEANUT BUTTER PERFECTION

This to-die-for pie makes the perfect ending to any meal.

Place the graham crackers in a plastic bag, and use a rolling pin to make crumbs. (There should be about 1½ cups of crumbs.) Pour the crumbs into a bowl, add the sugar and melted margarine, and stir well with a fork.

Pour the crumb mixture into a 9-inch pie plate, and press the mixture into the bottom and sides of the plate with the back of a large spoon. Refrigerate the crust for 30 minutes before filling it.

In a blender, purée the tofu, peanut butter, melted chocolate chips, and maple syrup until smooth. Cover the bottom of the chilled pie crust with thin slices of banana. Pour the tofu mixture over the banana slices, and chill for at least 2 hours.

8-10 chocolate graham crackers
  (4 sections per cracker)
¼ cup sugar
⅓ cup dairy-free margarine, melted
2 (12.3-oz.) pkgs. soft silken tofu
  (2 ⅔ cups)
¾ cup peanut butter
1½ cups semisweet chocolate
  chips, melted
1 tablespoon maple syrup
1 ripe banana, sliced

DESSERTS

Per servings: Calories 468, Protein 15 g, Fat 26 g, Carbohydrates 44 g, Calcium 63 mg, Fiber 6 g, Sodium 102 mg

KEY LIME PIE FILLING

You know this Floridian favorite is fabulous as a pie filling, but there's no need to bother with a crust! It also makes a terrific tangy pudding.

Yield: 8 servings

¼ cup fresh key lime juice
2½ cups soymilk
1 cup granulated sweetener of your choice
5 tablespoons cornstarch
2 teaspoons organic lime zest

Microwave Method: Whip all the ingredients together until smooth. Pour in a 2-quart glass measuring cup or bowl, and cook on HIGH for 10 minutes, stopping to whip every 2 minutes.

Stovetop Method: Whip all the ingredients together in a saucepan, and heat over moderate heat, stirring constantly until thick and creamy.

After the filling has cooked, pour it into a baked 9-inch pie crust or 8 serving dishes, and chill until firm. Top with Sweet Cream Topping, p. 24, and decorate with lime slices.

Per serving (filling only): Calories 139, Protein 2 g, Fat 1 g, Carbohydrates 30 g, Calcium 5 mg, Fiber 1 g, Sodium 9 mg

LUSCIOUS LEMON PIE

Do try the optional topping for this easy, creamy pie. One taste, and you'll realize that egg-based meringue isn't all it's cracked up to be!

Yield: 8 servings

Preheat the oven to 350°F.

Combine the filling ingredients together in a blender or food processor until very smooth. Pour this into the crust, and bake for 35 minutes. Cool the pie on a rack, then refrigerate.

To make the optional "meringue," mix the agar and water in a small saucepan, and let set for about 5 minutes. Stir over medium heat until it simmers, then allow to simmer 1 minute.

In a deep, medium bowl, beat the egg replacer and ¾ cup water with an electric or rotary egg beater until it resembles softly mounded egg whites. Beat in the sugar, vanilla, and lemon extract, then the cooked agar mixture. Beat well to distribute the agar evenly. When smooth and glossy, cool it in the refrigerator. It will firm up. Beat it again briefly, then pile the mixture around the edge of the pie, leaving the edge of the crust and the center showing. Make little peaks in the "meringue" with the back of a spoon. Refrigerate until ready to serve.

1 (9-inch) graham cracker crust

Filling:
1 lb. medium-firm tofu
¼ cup sugar
½ cup lemon juice (preferably fresh, but bottled will do)
2 tablespoons cornstarch
Zest of 1 large lemon, grated, or 2 teaspoons lemon extract

Optional "Meringue" Topping:
1⅓ teaspoons agar powder (or 2 tablespoons + 2 teaspoons agar flakes) mixed with ¼ cup cold water
½ cup powdered egg replacer
¾ cup cold water
½ cup sugar
4 teaspoons pure vanilla extract
½ teaspoon pure lemon extract

Per serving: Calories 309, Protein 11 g, Fat 12 g, Carbohydrates 38 g, Calcium 101 mg, Fiber 1 g, Sodium 260 mg

D
E
S
S
E
R
T
S

MINCED FRUIT TARTS

These elegant pastries are a hit at dinner parties. Keep the filling on hand for any time you need a special treat that's sure to impress.

Filling:
1½ lbs. raisins
1 lb. candied peel
1 lb. golden raisins (sultanas)
1 lb. currents
2 lbs. apples, chopped
1½ lbs. brown sugar
Rind and juice of 1 lemon and
   1 orange
1 oz. mixed spice
½ oz. nutmeg
1 cup brandy
1 lb. dairy-free margarine

Pastry:
9 tablespoons vegetable shortening
4 tablespoons water
Pinch of salt
2 cups all-purpose flour

Mix all the ingredients in a food processor. Put in a large bowl, cover, and stir every day for one week. Pack in canning jars, leaving one inch of space at the top. Cover the jars with waxed paper before putting the lids on. It will keep for a long time.

Place all the ingredients in a food processor, and process just enough to form a ball. Do not overprocess. Transfer the dough to a sheet of waxed paper, flatten into a circle, and refrigerate for 1 hour. Roll out the dough and cut circles for tarts.

Preheat the oven to 475°F. To assemble the tarts, roll the pastry dough circles out into rounds the size of the bottom of your muffin tins. Put the bottom round in the muffin tin, fill with minced fruit, and cover with the top round. Make a few small holes in the top with a fork. Bake for 20 minutes. Remove as you would muffins. Allow to cool. Sprinkle a little sugar on top before serving.

Per tart: Calories 492, Protein 3 g, Fat 17 g, Carbohydrates 76 g,
Calcium 78 mg, Fiber 5 g, Sodium 231 mg

TUTTI FRUITY PIE

A staple of raw foods restaurants, no-bake pies are a delicious way to savor the flavors of fresh summer fruits.

Place the sunflower seeds and almonds in a food processor, and blend until finely ground. Set aside. Place the dates or raisins in a food processor, and blend to form a paste. With the motor running, add the ground seeds and nuts through the feed tube. Blend until the mixture forms a ball.

Press the mixture evenly on the bottom and sides of a lightly oiled 8-inch pie pan. Chill.

Combine ⅔ of the strawberries and 1 banana in a food processor, and blend until the fruit is puréed. Set aside. Cut the remaining strawberries, banana, and kiwis into small slices. Spoon the sliced strawberries, banana, and kiwis and the pineapple chunks into the pie crust, pour the puréed mixture over the sliced fruit, and top with the coconut. Chill for 1 hour.

¼ cup sunflower seeds
1 cup almonds
1½ cups pitted dates or raisins
18-20 whole strawberries
2 bananas
2 kiwis
½ cup pineapple chunks
1 tablespoon grated coconut

DESSERTS

Per serving: Calories 284, Protein 5 g, Fat 13 g, Carbohydrates 36 g, Calcium 76 mg, Fiber 7 g, Sodium 12 mg

CHOCOLATE CHIP BROWNIE BARS

We're not quite sure whether these bars are more cake or brownie. Whatever you call them, they're positively scrumptious.

Yield: 24 bars

DESSERTS

1⅓ cups flour
½ teaspoon baking soda
½ cup dairy-free margarine, softened
1 cup sugar
3 tablespoons oil
1 (12.3 oz.) pkg. soft or firm silken tofu (1½ cups)
⅓ cup unsweetened cocoa powder
1 teaspoon vanilla extract
1 cup walnuts
1 cup semi-sweet chocolate chips
¾ cup coconut

Preheat the oven to 350°F. Combine the flour and baking soda, and set aside. Combine the margarine, sugar, and oil in a food processor, and process 2 minutes, or until light and fluffy. Add the tofu and process 2 minutes longer. Add the cocoa powder and vanilla, and process for a short time. Slowly add the dry mixture, processing periodically. Pour into a bowl and add the nuts, chocolate chips, and coconut. Pour the batter into a lightly oiled 9 x 12-inch baking pan. Bake for 25 minutes (check at 20 minutes).

Per bar: Calories 232, Protein 4 g, Fat 16 g, Carbohydrates 20 g, Calcium 38 mg, Fiber 2 g, Sodium 67 mg

CHOCOLATE CHIP COOKIES

Whether fresh from the oven or plucked from the cookie jar tomorrow, these cookies are equally yummy.

Yield: 5 dozen cookies

Heat the oven to 375°F. Combine the vegetable shortening, margarine, sugar, soymilk, and vanilla in a bowl. Beat at medium speed until creamy. Beat in the egg replacer. Combine the flour, salt, baking powder, and baking soda, and mix into the creamed mixture. Stir in the chips and nuts. Drop rounded tablespoons of dough 3 inches apart onto an unoiled baking sheet. Bake for 8-13 minutes.

½ cup vegetable shortening
¼ cup dairy-free margarine
1 cup light brown sugar
¼ cup granulated sugar
2 tablespoons soymilk
1 tablespoon vanilla
Egg replacer, equivalent to 1 egg
1¾ cups all-purpose flour
1 teaspoon salt
1¼ teaspoons baking soda
1 teaspoon baking powder
1 cup chocolate chips
1 cup pecan pieces

DESSERTS

Per cookie: Calories 73, Protein 1 g, Fat 4 g, Carbohydrates 7 g, Calcium 14 mg, Fiber 0 g, Sodium 71 mg

CRISPY RICE TREATS

These easy treats are great for kids' parties. They're also a nice surprise tucked into a brown bag lunch! Try adding dried fruit for a delicious variation.

Yield: about 32 treats

¾ cup peanut butter
¾ cup brown rice syrup
½ teaspoon vanilla
½ teaspoon cinnamon
¼ cup chopped peanuts
½ cup carob or semi-sweet chocolate chips
2 cups crispy rice cereal
Additional chopped peanuts or shredded coconut

Mix the peanut butter, rice syrup, vanilla, cinnamon, ¼ cup chopped peanuts, and carob chips together in a large bowl. Add the cereal, stirring gently until it is well-coated.

Place a small bowl of water near your work surface. Using wet hands, form the cereal mixture into walnut-sized balls, and roll the balls in chopped peanuts or shredded coconut. Place the balls in a container lined with waxed paper. Store at room temperature or in the freezer.

Per treat: Calories 94, Protein 2 g, Fat 4 g, Carbohydrates 10 g, Calcium 6 mg, Fiber 1 g, Sodium 15 mg

FUDGY COCOA MINT COOKIES

Zucchini make these chewy cookies marvelously moist—just don't tell your kids the secret "ingredient"! For variety, try vanilla, coffee, or coconut extract instead of peppermint.

Yield: 48 cookies

Preheat the oven to 350°F.

Mix the flour, cocoa, baking soda, and salt together in a bowl.

Beat the oil, sweetener, zucchini, and peppermint extract together with a mixer. Add the dry ingredients and beat until smooth. Fold in the walnuts.

Drop by tablespoonfuls onto cookie sheets, and bake for about 12 minutes.

3 cups unbleached or whole wheat flour or 1½ cups of each
¼ cup cocoa
2 teaspoons baking soda
¼ teaspoon salt
2 tablespoons oil
1½ cups granulated sweetener
2½ cups finely grated zucchini (⅜ lb.)
1 teaspoon peppermint extract
1 cup chopped walnuts (optional)

Per cookie: Calories 57, Protein 1 g, Fat 0 g, Carbohydrates 12 g, Calcium 14 mg, Fiber 1 g, Sodium 46 mg

JEAN'S PECAN BALLS

Reminiscent of Mexican wedding cookies, these treats are the perfect ending to a Southwestern fiesta—or a Northeastern tea party!

¼ lb. very soft dairy-free margarine (½ cup)
2 tablespoons plus ¼ cup confectioners' sugar
1 teaspoon water
1 teaspoon vanilla extract
1 cup flour
¾ cup crushed pecans

Preheat the oven to 350°F. Mix together the margarine, 2 tablespoons confectioners' sugar, water, vanilla, flour, and crushed pecans. Flour your hands and roll into 1-inch balls. Bake until delicately brown, about 20 minutes. About 3 minutes after removing from the oven, roll in the remaining confectioners' sugar.

Per ball: Calories 97, Protein 1 g, Fat 6 g, Carbohydrates 7 g, Calcium 13 mg, Fiber 0 g, Sodium 53 mg

DESSERTS

OATMEAL COOKIES

Your kids might frown over their morning oatmeal, but these delicious cookies are sure to make them smile.

Yield: 5 dozen cookies

Preheat the oven to 350°F. Blend the tofu until smooth and creamy. Pour into a bowl and mix with the oil, sweetener, and vanilla.

In another bowl, mix the oats, flour, baking powder, baking soda, and salt. Mix the dry ingredients into the wet ingredients along with the walnuts and raisins. Drop by heaping tablespoonfuls onto oiled cookie sheets, and bake for 15 minutes.

¾ cup soft tofu
1 cup oil
1½ cups liquid sweetener
1 tablespoon vanilla
4 cups rolled oats
2½ cups unbleached white flour
1 teaspoon baking powder
1 teaspoon baking soda
½ teaspoon salt
½ cup chopped walnuts
½ cup raisins

D
E
S
S
E
R
T
S

Per cookie: Calories 121, Protein 2 g, Fat 4 g, Carbohydrates 20 g,
Calcium 20 mg, Fiber 1 g, Sodium 40 mg

PEANUT BETTER BARS

A favorite at PETA picnics, these bars always disappear in record time.

6 cups corn flakes
1 cup light corn syrup
1 cup sugar
1½ cups peanut butter
1 (8-oz.) bag chocolate chips (2 bags
   if you are a chocolate lover)

Lightly oil an 8 x 10-inch cake pan, and place the corn flakes in the pan. Mix the corn syrup and sugar in a saucepan, and bring to a light boil. Remove from the heat, add the peanut butter, and mix until smooth. Pour the mixture over the corn flakes, and combine. In a double boiler or saucepan, melt the chocolate chips and pour over the top of the cereal mixture. Place in the refrigerator overnight to harden. The next day, cut and serve.

Per bar: Calories 80, Protein 2 g, Fat 4 g, Carbohydrates 10 g,
Calcium 22 mg, Fiber 1 g, Sodium 31 mg

RASPBERRY CRUMBLE BARS

The "berry" best bars you've ever tasted. Irresistible!

Yield: 15 pieces

Preheat the oven to 350°F. Oil a 9 x 13-inch pan.

In a large mixing bowl, mix the margarine, sugar, egg replacer, and vanilla together. In a small mixing bowl, mix the flour, baking powder, and shredded coconut together. Slowly add the dry mixture to the wet mixture. Press ⅔ of the dough into the oiled pan, and spread the preserves on top of it. Crumble the remaining dough with a fork. You may need to sprinkle the dough with flour so that small crumbs form. Sprinkle the crumbs on top of the preserves.

Bake 35-40 minutes until the edges are slightly browned, and enjoy!

¾ cup dairy-free margarine
1 cup sugar
Egg replacer, equivalent to 1 egg
1 teaspoon vanilla
2 cups + 1 tablespoon flour
½ tablespoon baking powder
1⅓ cups shredded coconut
1 small jar *seedless* raspberry preserves (apricot can also be used)

D
E
S
S
E
R
T
S

Per piece: Calories 358, Protein 3 g, Fat 21 g, Carbohydrates 37 g, Calcium 63 mg, Fiber 2 g, Sodium 168 mg

AMAZING APPLE AND DATE MOUSSE

Enjoying fresh fruits has never been so delicious!

D
E
S
S
E
R
T
S

1½ lb. apples, cored and diced
1-1½ tablespoons lemon juice
1 teaspoon lemon zest
3 tablespoons maple syrup
½ lb. fresh dates, pitted
1 teaspoon sesame seeds
Lemon balm, mint, or lemon
   geranium leaves to garnish

Cook the apples with the lemon juice, zest, and maple syrup until the fruit is soft. You may need to add a little water. Let cool.

In a blender, blend the dates and apples together until light and fluffy. Stir in the sesame seeds. Spoon the mousse into 4 dessert glasses, and chill. Garnish with fresh lemon balm, mint, or lemon geranium leaves.

Per serving: Calories 299, Protein 1 g, Fat 0 g, Carbohydrates 71 g, Calcium 54 mg, Fiber 10 g, Sodium 4 mg

CHOCOLATE PUDDING

Who would think that tofu could make such a creamy—and dreamy—dessert? The proof is in this phenomenal pudding

Yield: 4 cups

Combine all the ingredients in a food processor or blender, and blend until smooth and creamy. Pour into individual serving dishes or a baked pie shell. Chill until firm and serve.

1½ lbs. soft tofu
1¼ cups sugar
⅓ cup cocoa
¼ cup oil
1½ teaspoons vanilla
¼ teaspoon salt or soy sauce

Per ½ cup: Calories 254, Protein 8 g, Fat 11 g, Carbohydrates 33 g, Calcium 95 mg, Fiber 2 g, Sodium 74 mg

DESSERTS

Every day, 840 million people—including 200 million children—go hungry. If everyone ate a plant-based diet, we would have enough food to sustain 10 billion people—nearly twice the number of people on the planet.

COCONUT FLAN

This Oriental-inspired dessert would be the perfect ending for a meal featuring Szechuan Noodles (p. 135) or Hot and Spicy Lo Mein (p. 120). Try serving it with chunks of pineapple and fresh mint leaves for garnish.

Syrup:
5 tablespoons granulated
   sweetener
3 tablespoons water

Pudding:
⅔ cup crumbled firm or medium-
   firm tofu
2 tablespoons granulated
   sweetener
1 tablespoon of the syrup (above)
½ teaspoon coconut extract
Pinch of salt
2½ cups soymilk or other nondairy
   milk
1½ tablespoons agar flakes,
   or ¼ teaspoon agar powder

To make the syrup, bring the water and sweetener to a boil over low heat in a small saucepan with a heavy bottom. Simmer, uncovered, for 5 minutes. Remove from the heat.

Working quickly, place the tofu, 2 tablespoons sweetener, 1 tablespoon of the syrup, the coconut extract, and salt in a blender. Set this aside and pour the remaining syrup evenly into 6 custard molds. Rotate each one to coat the base and sides with the syrup. Set aside.

Into the same saucepan, combine the nondairy milk and agar. Bring this quickly to a boil, stirring constantly, then reduce the heat, and simmer for 5 minutes. Continue stirring. Add this hot milk mixture to the ingredients in the blender, and immediately blend it into a smooth cream. Stir down the bubbles.

Pour the blended mixture into the coated molds, and skim off any remaining foam. Cover the molds with plastic wrap, and refrigerate them until serving time.

To unmold the puddings, dip the bottom of each mold briefly into boiling water, then remove the plastic wrap and turn upside down on a dessert plate. The pudding should slide out easily. Pour any syrup left in the bottom of the mold over the pudding.

Decorate each plate with fruit and mint or lemon balm sprigs.

Per serving: Calories 117, Protein 4 g, Fat 2 g, Carbohydrates 21 g, Calcium 33 mg, Fiber 1 g, Sodium 14 mg

Animals raised for food are dosed with half of all the antibiotics produced in the United States. But up to 80 percent of the drugs farmers administer to animals are used to accelerate growth, not to treat illnesses.

CRISPY WRAPPED BAKED BANANAS

These are very easy to make, and the contrast between the hot, crispy, baked bananas and the cold, creamy, nondairy vanilla dessert is delicious! Serve immediately after baking.

Yield: 6 servings

3 whole sheets of phyllo pastry
6 medium-ripe bananas
Lemon juice
2 tablespoons dark granulated
   sweetener
1½ teaspoons coconut extract
Apple juice
1½ pints nondairy, vanilla frozen
   dessert of your choice

If the phyllo sheets are frozen, thaw them; cut them in half vertically, and keep well-covered. Peel the bananas and brush them with lemon juice to keep from discoloring.

Preheat the oven to 400°F.

To make each wrapped banana, place one banana at the bottom (short end) of half a phyllo sheet, and sprinkle the banana with 1 teaspoon of sweetener and ¼ teaspoon coconut extract. Roll the dough over it once, then fold in the outer edges, and keep rolling away from you. Place the wrapped bananas on a lightly oiled cookie sheet, and brush the tops with apple juice. Bake for 15 to 20 minutes, or until golden and crispy. Serve immediately with a scoop of the frozen dessert on each plate.

Per serving: Calories 310, Protein 3 g, Fat 8 g, Carbohydrates 57 g, Calcium 27 mg, Fiber 3 g, Sodium 109 mg

OLDE-FASHIONED PLUM PUDDING

Start a new tradition by serving this old favorite at your next holiday dinner.

Yield: 12 servings

Mix all the pudding ingredients together, and divide among 6 individual pudding bowls that have been lightly brushed with oil. Cover the bowls with parchment paper, tie each one in a clean dishcloth, and submerge in gently boiling water for one hour. Turn out the pudding on individual serving plates, dust lightly with powdered sugar, and garnish with holly. Serve with Orange-Brandy Sauce.

Combine the orange juice and zest with the brandy in a small saucepan, and bring to a boil. Add a little arrowroot and stir until the sauce is thickened.

Pudding:
¾ cup ground almonds
¾ cup chopped prunes
½ cup chopped walnuts
½ cup toasted chopped almonds
½ cup raisins
½ cup chopped maraschino cherries
½ cup dairy-free margarine
2 cups whole wheat bread crumbs
½ teaspoon cinnamon
½ teaspoon nutmeg
Pinch of cloves
½ cup orange juice
¼ cup brandy

Orange Brandy Sauce:
¾ cup orange juice
4 tablespoons grated orange zest
¼ cup + 2 tablespoons brandy
Pinch of arrowroot

Per serving: Calories 300, Protein 5 g, Fat 18 g, Carbohydrates 23 g, Calcium 69 mg, Fiber 4 g, Sodium 132 mg

D
E
S
S
E
R
T
S

CHOCOLATE "NICE CREAM"

Bye-bye, Ben & Jerry's—creamy, chocolate "nice cream" is one of the coolest treats you'll ever want to eat!

2 lbs. soft tofu
2 cups nondairy milk
1 cup vegetable oil
2 cups brown sugar
½ cup cocoa
2 tablespoons vanilla
¼ teaspoon salt
½ cup creamy peanut butter
  (optional)

Blend all the ingredients and pour into an ice-cream maker. Follow the manufacturer's instructions, serve, and enjoy.

Variation: Don't add the peanut butter until the last few minutes of freezing in order to get a ripple effect.

Per cup: Calories 336, Protein 7 g, Fat 22 g, Carbohydrates 27 g, Calcium 107 mg, Fiber 2 g, Sodium 64 mg

STRAWBERRY "NICE CREAM"

Don't have a cow, man! Be a bovine buddy instead, and try this delectable dairy-free frozen dessert.

Blend all the ingredients, except the strawberries, until smooth. Add the chopped strawberries, and blend for only a few more seconds. Pour into an ice cream maker, follow the manufacturer's instructions, serve, and enjoy.

2 lbs. soft tofu
1 cup nondairy milk
2 cups brown sugar
1⅓ cups vegetable oil
Juice of 2 lemons
2 tablespoons vanilla
¼ teaspoon salt
1 tablespoon strawberry flavoring or extract
2 pints fresh strawberries

D
E
S
S
E
R
T
S

Per serving: Calories 383, Protein 6 g, Fat 26 g, Carbohydrates 28 g, Calcium 108 mg, Fiber 2 g, Sodium 60 mg

ARTHUR AND GUINEVERE

In 1988, we had an early fall, and, as it became colder, we decided to let our turkeys, Arthur and Guinevere, live in our breezeway which is enclosed and heated. It is just off the kitchen and we use it like a room in our house. We began to get to know our birds better.

We noticed that Arthur and Guinevere take an interest in everything that goes on in front of our house. As we are directly across from the entrance to a college playing field, and we have many children in the neighborhood, there is always a lot happening. It intrigued us, the way the birds were always at the window observing and seemingly fascinated by all the human activities and occasionally adding their own vocal contribution.

As I spend several hours a day in the kitchen with the radio going, I found that there are certain kinds of music the birds seem to prefer. Arthur gobbles indignantly at loud, wild music or talk but listens quietly to soft, slow sounds.

Guinevere is especially fond of flute music. One day, just after I had given her and Arthur some fresh greens, a flute solo came on the radio in the kitchen. Guinevere stopped eating (something I had never seen her do with greens in front of her), came to the foot of the stairs, listened for a moment or two, and began a sweet trilling—a sound unfamiliar to me in the years we had known her. As I watched and listened, entranced, she began to sway from side to side in time with the music. I quickly called to Ted, a family friend who was visiting, and asked, "What is she doing?" I could not believe what I was seeing. Ted answered, "It's obvious. She's singing and dancing!" When the music stopped, she stopped and went back to her snack.

Arthur and Guinevere get along well together, and at night they sleep in close contact with each other. If Arthur is blocking the doorway, and Guinevere wants to go out, she waits quietly until Arthur feels like moving.

Guinevere likes to be scratched gently under her wings. When she wants this attention, her technique is to walk in front of me and flop down, blocking my movement. The sound she makes when I oblige her is an unmistakable "Ahhh."

Sometimes Guinevere sleeps on the stoop just outside the kitchen door, the way a dog or cat will do, trying to get as close as possible to a beloved master. If the door is left open, she will come into the kitchen, and, when I open the refrigerator, she helps herself to the greens I have left for her.

I admit to being fascinated by these two individuals. The work and expense involved is little to pay for the awesome experience of communicating with two unique and lovable personalities.

—excerpted from "Our House Turkeys"
by Marion Wickersham

DRINKS

"Now I can look at you in peace. I don't eat you anymore."
—Franz Kafka, admiring a fish

CAROB-PEANUT BUTTER SMOOTHIE

Try this simple smoothie the next time you have a snack attack. With peanut butter, how can you go wrong?

Yield: I large or 2 small servings

1 medium banana, cut into chunks
  and frozen
1 cup soymilk
4 teaspoons carob powder
2 tablespoons peanut butter
1 teaspoon maple syrup

Place all the ingredients in a blender, and purée until smooth.

Per small serving: Calories 214, Protein 8 g, Fat 9 g, Carbohydrates 24 g, Calcium 32 mg, Fiber 5 g, Sodium 21 mg

FRUIT SMOOTHIE

Combine any of your favorite fruits with soymilk to make a splendid blended drink. Freezing the fruits first makes smoothies extra thick and creamy.

Yield: I large or 2 small servings

1 cup soymilk
1 medium banana, cut into chunks
  and frozen
½ cup frozen fruit (strawberries,
  blueberries, chopped apricots,
  pitted cherries—whatever you
  like!)
1 tablespoon maple syrup
Dash of cinnamon

Place all the ingredients in a blender, and purée until smooth.

Per small serving: Calories 128, Protein 4 g, Fat 2 g, Carbohydrates 23 g, Calcium 24 mg, Fiber 3 g, Sodium 17 mg

LASSI

Lassi is an Indian drink traditionally made with yogurt or buttermilk, but this version is so delicious no one will know you've dumped the dairy—unless you tell them!

Yield: 6 to 8 servings

Place the fruit of your choice, liquid of your choice, additional ingredients, and any optional ingredients in the blender container. (Make sure that your blender can take ice cubes without damaging it.) Blend until the ice is well ground up and the mixture is frothy. Pour into glasses and serve immediately.

*To make a fruit nectar to use in lassi, soak ½ cup dried apricots, peaches, or papayas in 2 cups pineapple juice until soft. Whiz in a blender until smooth. Use this in place of canned apricot nectar or frozen juice concentrate when fresh fruit is not available.

TOP TIP: You can also use low-fat tofu in this recipe and still get delicious results.

Fruit (use ONE of the following):
1⅓ cups ripe peeled and chopped mango, papaya, or pineapple,
or 1 cup frozen peach cocktail concentrate, or pineapple or papaya juice concentrate,
or 1 cup apricot nectar or fruit nectar*

Liquid (use ONE of the following):
2⅔ cups cold water + ¼ cup liquid sweetener,
or 2 cups cold water + ¾ cup frozen apple juice concentrate,
or 3 cups fruit juice of your choice

Additional Ingredients:
1 cup tofu
12 ice cubes
¼ cup lemon juice

Optional Ingredients:
2 teaspoons dairy-free acidophilus powder
½ teaspoon coconut extract or ground cardamom, nutmeg, or ginger

D R I N K S

Per serving: Calories 94, Protein 4 g, Fat 2 g, Carbohydrates 16 g, Calcium 42 mg, Fiber 1 g, Sodium 4 mg

MEXICAN-STYLE HOT CHOCOLATE

Mexican hot chocolate is a rich concoction of whipped milk, melted chocolate, sugar, and just a hint of almonds and cinnamon. Blending tofu and cocoa powder results in a fabulous, frothy chocolate—minus the fat!

Yield: 4 servings

3 cups boiling water
½ lb. firm or medium-firm tofu
¼ cup sugar or other sweetener, to taste
¼ cup unsweetened cocoa powder
1 teaspoon pure vanilla extract
½ teaspoon pure almond extract
¼ teaspoon salt
¼ teaspoon ground cinnamon

Mix all the ingredients in a blender until smooth and foamy. Pour into hot mugs and serve immediately.

For a mocha version, use hot coffee or coffee substitute instead of water.

Per serving: Calories 111, Protein 5 g, Fat 2 g, Carbohydrates 14 g, Calcium 68 mg, Fiber 3 g, Sodium 139 mg

DRINKS

EGGLESS "EGGNOG"

Forget what the calendar says: This eggs-cellent eggless "eggnog" is a refreshing drink any time of the year! You can make the "eggnog" mix ahead of time, then blend it with the ice cubes just before serving.

Yield: 12 servings

Place the crumbled tofu and soymilk in a blender with the sweetener and salt. Blend until very smooth. Scrape this into a large bowl or pitcher, and whisk in the water, rum or brandy, and vanilla. Mix well, cover, and refrigerate until serving time.

To serve, blend half of the mixture in the blender with 12 of the ice cubes until frothy. Repeat with the other half. Serve in glasses with nutmeg sprinkled on top.

2 (12.3 oz.) pkgs. extra-firm silken tofu (3 cups) crumbled
2⅓ cups soymilk, or other plain, nondairy milk
½ cup granulated sweetener, or 1 cup liquid sweetener
¼ teaspoon salt
1¼ cups cold water
1¼ cups rum or brandy (or use apple juice with rum or brandy flavoring, to taste)
5-6 teaspoons pure vanilla extract
24 ice cubes
Freshly grated nutmeg

Per serving: Calories 130, Protein 5 g, Fat 1 g, Carbohydrates 13 g, Calcium 18 mg, Fiber 1 g, Sodium 70 mg

JUICY JUNGLE PUNCH

Give boring beverages the boot. This easy punch will be the life of any party!

Yield: 3 quarts

2 cups mashed banana
1 (20-oz.) can crushed pineapple,
 undrained
1 (6-oz.) jar maraschino cherries,
 drained and chopped
2 cups orange juice
1 tablespoon lemon juice
½ cup sugar
1 qt. ginger ale, chilled

Combine all the ingredients, except the ginger ale, and stir well. Freeze until firm.

To serve, partially thaw the punch mixture, and place it in a large punch bowl. Break the mixture into chunks. Add the ginger ale and stir until the punch is slushy.

Per cup: Calories 146, Protein 1 g, Fat 0 g, Carbohydrates 35 g,
Calcium 16 mg, Fiber 1 g, Sodium 7 mg

STRAWBERRY LIME FREEZE

Eat it straight out of the blender with a spoon, or let it set a bit, and sip through a straw. Either way, this tart treat is a must for summer afternoons on the veranda.

Yield: 2 cups

1 (16-oz.) pkg. frozen strawberries
Juice of 3 limes
2 tablespoons sugar
¼ cup water

Mix the ingredients in a blender until thick and smooth. Pour into decorative glasses and decorate with mint sprigs.

Per ½ cup: Calories 63, Protein 1 g, Fat 0 g, Carbohydrates 15 g,
Calcium 18 mg, Fiber 2 g, Sodium 2 mg

D R I N K S

TASTE OF THE TROPICS SMOOTHIE

Take your taste buds to the tropics with this exotic drink!

Yield: 2 servings

Place all the ingredients, except for the toasted coconut, in a blender, and purée until smooth. Pour into two tall glasses, and garnish with a little toasted coconut, if desired.

½ lb. soft tofu
1 very ripe banana, cut into chunks and frozen
1 mango, peeled, cut into chunks, and frozen
1½ cups pineapple-orange juice
Dash of coconut extract
Maple syrup, to taste (optional)
Toasted coconut for garnish (optional)

Per serving: Calories 289, Protein 10 g, Fat 5 g, Carbohydrates 49 g, Calcium 153 mg, Fiber 4 g, Sodium 13 mg

At the turn of the century, there were only two tofu manufacturers in the United States. Today, there are 200.

WARM WINTER WINE

Take the chill off holiday guests with this warm and spicy wine.

Yield: 3 to 4 servings

1 (750 ml.) bottle red wine
¼ teaspoon ground nutmeg
½ teaspoon ground ginger
3 cinnamon sticks
2 tablespoons maple syrup
Splash of brandy

In a large pan, gently heat the wine and spices with the maple syrup. Bring just to a boil, then remove from the heat. Stir in the brandy and serve.

Per serving: Calories 24, Protein 0 g, Fat 0 g, Carbohydrates 4 g,
Calcium 7 mg, Fiber 0 g, Sodium 1 mg

D
R
I
N
K
S

GLOSSARY OF INGREDIENTS

Agar—A gelling agent made from sea vegetables that can be used in place of gelatin in molded salads and desserts. Agar is available in flakes or as a powder. Sold in health food stores.

Arborio rice—A short-grain white rice that is traditionally used to make risotto, a creamy Northern Italian rice dish. Available in regular grocery stores.

Arrowroot—A dried and powdered tropical plant root that is used as a thickening agent. Arrowroot can be substituted for other thickeners, like cornstarch or kuzu, in equal amounts. Available in health food stores.

Balsamic vinegar—A slightly sweet Italian vinegar made from grapes. Available in regular grocery stores.

Barley—A mild, chewy grain that is available in hulled and pearl varieties. Hulled barley is more nutritious than pearl barley, from which most of the bran, in addition to the inedible hulls, has been removed. Sold in regular grocery stores and health food stores.

Bean sprouts—The edible shoots of beans that have been soaked in water. Often the term "bean sprouts" refers to mung bean sprouts, which are used in many Chinese dishes. Available in regular grocery stores.

Brown rice syrup—A natural sweetener made by fermenting cooked rice and barley enzymes. Brown rice syrup can be substituted for honey, but because it is less sweet, you may need to use a little more. Available in health food stores.

Brown rice vinegar—A Japanese vinegar made from fermented brown rice. Available in some regular grocery stores, health food stores, and Oriental markets.

Bulgur—A nutty-tasting grain that is made by steaming, drying, and cracking whole wheat. Bulgur is used in many Middle Eastern recipes, including tabouleh. Available in some regular grocery stores and health food stores.

Capers—Pickled flower buds that are used as a condiment in savory dishes. Available in regular grocery stores and gourmet shops.

Carob—The dried, roasted, and ground pods of the carob tree. Carob powder has a chocolate-like flavor but, unlike chocolate, contains no caffeine. Carob chips are also available. Sold in health food stores.

Cashew butter—A creamy paste similar to peanut butter that is made from finely ground, roasted cashews. Many markets also carry almond butter, hazelnut butter, and other nut and seed butters. You can also make your own by grinding nuts in a food processor. Available in health food stores and gourmet markets.

Chipotle chilies—Dried and smoked jalapeño peppers. They can be found whole, powdered, or canned. Available in regular grocery stores and gourmet shops.

Cilantro—Fresh leaves of the coriander plant. Cilantro is often used in Mexican, Indian, and Oriental cooking. Available in regular grocery stores.

Coconut milk—A milk-like liquid strained from grated coconut that has been boiled in water. Low-fat and regular varieties are available. Sold in some regular grocery stores, health food stores, and Oriental markets.

Couscous—A North African grain that is made by steaming and drying durum wheat (the wheat used for making many types of pasta). Couscous is very versatile and can be used for hot cereals, savory grain dishes, and desserts. Available in some regular grocery stores and health food stores.

Curry paste—A spicy paste containing puréed chili peppers and dried herbs and spices often used to flavor Indian and Oriental dishes. Available in some regular grocery stores and Oriental and Indian markets

Egg-free mayonnaise—Mayonnaise made with vegetable oils instead of eggs. Low-fat and regular varieties are available. Sold in health food stores.

Egg replacer—A combination of leavening agents and starches used to replace eggs in baked goods. Available in health food stores.

Gingerroot—A light brown, knobby, aromatic root that can be sliced, minced, or grated and used in everything from savory stir-fries to spicy gingerbread. In a pinch, ½ tsp. ground ginger can be substituted for 1 Tbsp. fresh gingerroot. Available in regular grocery stores.

Instant gluten flour—Instant gluten flour or powder (also known as vital wheat gluten or "Do-Pep") is made from the gluten in wheat. Do not confuse this with high-gluten wheat flour, which is used as is to make bread. Instant gluten flour can be mixed with cold liquid and cooked in flavored broth to make meat substitutes. Cooked gluten is known by its Japanese name *seitan*. Available in regular grocery stores.

Jicama—A Central American root vegetable with light brown skin and white, slightly sweet flesh. Jicama can be eaten raw or cooked. Available in regular grocery stores and Mexican markets.

Kalamata olives—Black olives that are marinated in a wine-vinegar mixture and are often used as a condiment in Greek dishes. Available in regular grocery stores and gourmet shops.

Kelp and kombu powders—Powders made from dried sea vegetables that give foods a slightly "fishy" flavor. Available in health food stores and Oriental markets.

Leeks—Long members of the onion family that, like scallions or green onions, have green tops and white bottoms. Available in regular grocery stores.

Liquid smoke—A liquid seasoning made by capturing the smoke from burning hickory wood. Liquid smoke gives food a smoky flavor and can be used in dishes that are traditionally seasoned with meat, such as split pea soup. Available in regular grocery stores.

Marmite—A dark, salty paste with a "beefy" flavor, also known as yeast extract. It is a popular spread in England and Australia. Available in some health food stores and gourmet markets.

Mirin—A low-alcohol Japanese cooking wine brewed from sweet brown rice. Available in some regular grocery stores, health food stores, and Oriental markets.

Miso—A salty fermented soybean paste that adds a rich flavor to soups, sauces, and spreads. Light-colored misos are more mellow and less salty than the dark, red, or brown varieties, which are generally used to season heartier dishes. Available in health food stores and Oriental markets.

Mung beans—Tiny pea-shaped beans that are native to India and are often used to make dal. Available in health food stores and Indian markets.

Mushrooms—Edible fungi that are sold both fresh and dried. Some of the mushrooms used in this book include white button (the most common supermarket variety), oyster (small, oyster-shaped mushrooms with a delicate flavor), and portobello (mature cremini mushrooms with a more intense flavor). Shiitake, porcini, and chanterelle mushrooms are also becoming increasingly popular. Available in regular grocery stores and gourmet shops.

Nutritional yeast—A cheesy-tasting food yeast, rich in B vitamins, protein, and other nutrients, that is grown on a molasses base. Nutritional yeast is available in flakes or as a powder; in recipes, twice as much flaked nutritional yeast can be substituted for the powdered form. Some brands contain whey, a cheese byproduct, so read product labels carefully. Available in health food stores.

Oat flour—Can be made easily and inexpensively in a dry blender by processing rolled or quick oatmeal until pulverized. Store in a tightly covered container in your freezer.

Pepperoncinis—Spicy Greek peppers that are marinated in a vinegar brine and used as a condiment. Available in regular grocery stores and gourmet shops.

Phyllo pastry—A paper-thin pastry used in Greek and Middle Eastern foods like spanikopita and bakhlava; also called filo. Available in regular grocery stores.

Pine nuts—Small, sweet-flavored nuts that are often roasted and used in pestos and sauces or as a garnish; also known as pignolia. Available in some regular grocery stores and gourmet markets.

Poblano peppers—Large, mild chili peppers that are often roasted and stuffed. Available in some regular grocery stores and Mexican markets.

Rice wine vinegar—Made from Oriental rice wine.

Rutabaga—A large root vegetable with brown skin and a flavorful yellow-orange flesh. Available in regular grocery stores.

Scotch bonnet peppers—Small yellow chili peppers native to Jamaica. Scotch bonnets are extremely hot, so they should be used judiciously. Available in some regular grocery stores and Mexican markets.

Seitan—A meat alternative made of wheat gluten; also known as "wheat meat." Instant gluten flour mixes, used to make seitan, are also available. Sold in health food stores.

Sesame meal—Ground roasted sesame seeds. You can make this at home by toasting the seeds in a dry skillet and pulverizing them in a blender. Just a small amount used in a recipe will provide a rich, nutty flavor without adding a lot of fat.

Sesame oil—A dark-colored oil expressed from sesame seeds that is often used in Oriental recipes. Available in some regular grocery stores, health food stores, and Oriental markets.

Shallots—Small bulbs with multiple cloves, like garlic, that have a mild onion flavor. Available in regular grocery stores.

Soba noodles—Japanese noodles made from buckwheat flour. Available in health food stores and Oriental markets.

Soy flour—A protein-rich flour milled from toasted soybeans that gives baked goods a hearty texture. Available in health food stores.

Soymilk—A cow's milk substitute made from ground and boiled soybeans.

Soymilk is available in a variety of flavors; rice and oat milks are other nondairy options. Sold in some regular grocery stores and health food stores.

Soymilk powder--A powder that makes an instant soymilk when mixed with water. Soymilk made from powder is an economical alternative to ready-made nondairy milks. Available in health food stores.

Szechuan hot bean paste—A popular Chinese condiment, also known as Chinese chili bean paste. Available in health food stores, Oriental markets, and gourmet shops.

Tahini—A nutty-flavored paste made from sesame seeds. Available in some regular grocery stores and health food stores.

Tamari—A wheat-free soy sauce made from soybeans, salt, and water. Available in health food stores and Oriental markets.

Tapioca—A starch that is derived from the root of a tropical plant and used as a thickening agent. Available in regular grocery stores.

Tempeh—A meat alternative made from fermented soybeans. Some varieties of tempeh also contain grains or other types of beans. Available in health food stores.

Textured vegetable protein—Small, shredded chunks of soybean-derived protein with a hearty, chewy texture. Available in health food stores.

Thai red chili paste—A popular, spicy, slightly sweet Thai condiment. Look for varieties without fish sauce. Available in Oriental markets.

Tofu—A versatile, high-protein food made from soybeans and available in a variety of textures; also known as bean curd. Soft tofu is a good dairy substitute and can be blended to make creamy dressings, dips, and desserts. Firm and extra-firm tofu are often used as meat substitutes and will hold their shape when stir-fried or baked. Silken tofu comes in shelf-stable, aseptic packages and is also available in soft and firm varieties. Sold in many regular grocery stores, health food stores, and Oriental markets.

Udon noodles—Japanese noodles made from wheat flour, rice flour, or a combination of the two. Available in health food stores and Oriental markets.

Ume (or umeboshi) plum vinegar—A Japanese vinegar made from the brine used to pickle umeboshi plums. Available in health food stores and Oriental markets.

Vegan cheese—A nut- or soy-based substitute for cheese. Nondairy cheeses are sold in both blocks or slices and are available in a variety of flavors. Finely grated parmesan-flavored soy "cheese" is also available. Many brands contain casein or other milk proteins, so read product labels carefully. Available in health food stores.

Vegetable bouillon cubes—Small cubes of evaporated seasoned vegetable stock. Vegetable bouillon cubes reconstituted in water can be substituted for broth in equal amounts. Available in health food stores.

Vegetable broth—A flavorful broth made by slowly simmering a variety of vegetables in water. Canned vegetable broth is available in many regular grocery stores and health food stores.

Vegetable broth powder—A flavorful powder that, when mixed with water, makes an instant vegetable broth. Available in health food stores.

Vegetarian "meats"—Ready-made meat alternatives made from a variety of plant foods, including soybeans, wheat gluten, and grated vegetables. Health food stores and, increasingly, many mainstream supermarkets carry everything from soy-based burgers and hot dogs to sausage substitutes, vegetarian "bacon" bits, and even phony "bologna."

Vegetarian Worcestershire sauce—Worcestershire sauce made without the anchovies found in traditional varieties. Available in health food stores, or see page 25.

Vital wheat gluten—see *instant gluten flour*.

RESOURCES

VEGETARIAN FOOD

Allergy Resources
557 Burbank St., Suite K
Broomfield, CO 80020
Tel.: 800-USE-FLAX
Fax: 303-438-0700
Markets alternative ingredients
for those who are allergic to
common foods such as wheat,
eggs, and dairy.

Gold Mine Natural Food
Company
3419 Hancock St.
San Diego, CA 92110-4307
Tel.: 800-475-FOOD
Fax: 619-296-9756
Specializes in macrobiotic,
organic, and Earth-wise prod-
ucts for people and home.

Good Taste Vegetarian Food
Imports
77 Columbia St., 17L
New York, NY 10002
Tel.: 212-228-1803
Fax: 212-673-7260
Imports, among other things,
Shin-Der products, makers of
faux fish. Send a self-addressed,
stamped envelope for a catalog.

Harvest Direct, Inc.
P.O. Box 988
Knoxville, TN 37901-0988
Tel.: 800-835-2867
Fax: 423-523-3372
Provides quality convenience
foods such as soups, entrées,
and baking mixes.

Mail Order Catalog
P.O. Box 180
Summertown, TN 38483
Tel.: 800-695-2241
Fax: 615-964-3518
Carries textured vegetable pro-
tein (some of it organic), nutri-
tional yeast, instant gluten flour,
soymilk powder.

Mountain Ark Trading Co.
799 Old Leicester Hwy.
Asheville, NC 28806
Tel.: 800-643-8909
Fax: 704-252-9479
Offers a wide variety of foods
like grains, non-dairy beverages, tempeh, sea vegetables,
and entrée mixes.

Natural Lifestyles Supplies
16 Lookout Dr.
Asheville, NC 28804-3330
Tel.: 800-752-2775
Fax: 704-252-3386
Offers a large selection of organ-
ic foods.

Pangea
7829 Woodmont Ave.
Bethesda, MD 20814
Tel.: 301-652-3181
Fax: 301-652-0442
Carries vegan marshmallows,
leather alternatives, vegan
chocolate and jello, cruelty-free
body care products, and more.

Walnut Acres
Walnut Acres Rd.
Penns Creek, PA 17862
Tel.: 800-433-3998
Fax: 717-837-1146
Most food items for sale at
Walnut Acres are grown or pro-
duced in-house, and many are
organic.

Grains, Rice, and Legumes

Beans and Beyond
818 Jefferson St.
Oakland, CA 94607
Tel.: 800-845-BEAN
Fax: 916-443-2241

Chieftan Wild Rice Company
P.O. Box 550
1210 Basswood Ave.
Spooner, WI 54801
Tel.: 800-262-6368
Fax: 715-635-6415

Natural Way Mills, Inc.
Route 2, Box 37
Middle River, MN 56737
Tel.: 218-222-3677
Fax: 218-222-3408

Baking Supplies and Bread

The King Arthur Flour Baker's
Catalogue
P.O. Box 876
Norwich, VT 05055-0876
Tel.: 800-827-6836
Fax: 800-343-3002

Mill City Bakery
974 Seventh St. W.
St. Paul, MN 55102
Tel.: 800-873-6844
Fax: 612-224-5634

Fruit and Vegetables

Delftree Farm
234 Union St.
North Adams, MA 01247
Tel.: 800-243-3742
Fax: 413-664-4908

Diamond Organics
P.O. Box 2159
Freedom, CA 95019
Tel.: 800-922-2396
Fax: 888-888-6777

Fruit and Vegetables (cont.)

Maine Coast Sea Vegetables
R.R. 1, Box 78
Franklin, ME 04634
Tel.: 207-565-2907
Fax: 207-565-2144

South Tex Organics
6 Betty Dr.
Mission, TX 78572
Tel.: 210-585-1040
Fax: 210-581-4540

Wood Prairie Farm
49 Kinney Rd.
Bridgewater, ME 04735
Tel.: 800-829-9765
Fax: 800-300-6494

Seeds for Change
P.O. Box 15700
Santa Fe, NM 87506
Tel.: 888-762-7333
Fax: 888-329-4762

Herbs and Spices

Frontier Cooperative Herbs
3021 78th St., P.O. Box 299
Norway, IA 52318
Tel.: 800-786-1388
Fax: 800-717-4372

Nature's Herb Company
1010 46th St.
Emeryville, CA 94608
Tel.: 510-601-0700
Fax: 510-601-7026

Penzey's, Ltd., Spice House
P.O. Box 933
Muskego, WI 53150
Tel.: 414-574-0277
Fax: 414-679-7878

International Fare

Jyoti Cuisine India
P.O. Box 516
Berwyn, PA 19312
Tel.: 610-296-4620
Fax: 610-889-0492

The Oriental Pantry
423 Great Rd.
Acton, MA 01720
Tel.: 800-828-0368
Fax: 617-275-4506

Substitutions for Meat and Other Animal Products

Lumen Foods
409 Scott St.
Lake Charles, LA 70601
Tel.: 800-256-2253
Fax: 318-436-1769

Whitewave, Inc.
1990 N. 57th Ct.
Boulder, CO 80301
Tel.: 800-488-9283
Fax: 303-443-3925

Vegetarian Groups

American Vegan Society
501 Old Harding Hwy.
Malaga, NJ 08328
Tel.: 609-694-2887

EarthSave International
706 Fredrick St.
Santa Cruz, CA 95062-2205
Tel.: 408-423-4069

Farm Animal Reform
Movement
P.O. Box 30654
Bethesda, MD 20824
Tel.: 301-530-1737

Food Animal Concerns Trust
P.O. Box 14599
Chicago, IL 60614
Tel.: 312-525-4952

North American Vegetarian
Society
P.O. Box 72
Dolgeville, NY 13329
Tel.: 518-568-7970

People for the Ethical Treatment
of Animals
501 Front St.
Norfolk, VA 23510
Tel.: 757-622-PETA

Physicians Committee for
Responsible Medicine
5100 Wisconsin Ave. N.W., #404
Washington, DC 20016
Tel.: 202-686-2216

Pure Food Campaign
860 Highway 61
Little Marais, MN 55614
Tel.: 218-226-4164

United Poultry Concerns
P.O. Box 59367
Potomac, MD 20859
Tel.: 301-948-2406

Vegan Outreach
10410 Forbes Rd.
Pittsburgh, PA 15235
Tel.: 412-247-3527

Vegetarian Resource Group
P.O. Box 1463
Baltimore, MD 21203
Tel.: 410-366-8343

COOKBOOKS

Bates, Dorothy R.
The Holiday Diet Cookbook
The Book Publishing Company
Summertown, Tenn., 1994

Batt, Eva
Vegan Cookery
Thorsons Publishers, Ltd.
Rochester, Vt., 1985

Bernstein, Neil
*Chef Neil's International
Vegetarian Cookbook*
The Book Publishing Company
Summertown, Tenn., 1995

Bloomfield, Barb
Fabulous Beans
The Book Publishing Company
Summertown, Tenn., 1994

Davis, Karen
*Instead of Chicken, Instead of
Turkey: A Poultryless "Poultry"
Potpourri*
The Book Publishing Company
Summertown, Tenn., 1993

Diamond, Marilyn
The American Vegetarian Cookbook
Warner Books
New York, 1990

Grogan, Bryanna
20 Minutes to Dinner
The Book Publishing Company
Summertown, Tenn., 1997

Hagler, Louise
Lighten Up! With Louise Hagler
The Book Publishing Company
Summertown, Tenn., 1995

Hagler, Louise
Soyfoods Cookery
The Book Publishing Company
Summertown, Tenn., 1996

Leshane, Patricia
*Vegetarian Cooking for People
With Diabetes*
The Book Publishing Company
Summertown, Tenn., 1994

PETA and Ingrid Newkirk
The Compassionate Cook
Warner Books, A Time Warner
Company
New York, 1993

Pitchford, Polly and Delia
Quigley
*Cookin' Healthy With One Foot
Out the Door: Quick Meals for
Fast Times*
The Book Publishing Company
Summertown, Tenn., 1994

Raymond, Jennifer
The Peaceful Palate
The Book Publishing Company
Summertown, Tenn., 1992

Sass, Lorna J.
*Recipes From an Ecological
Kitchen: Healthy Meals for You
and the Planet*
William Morrow and Company,
Inc.
New York, 1992

Scott, David and Claire
Golding
*The Vegan Diet: True Vegetarian
Cookery*
Rider and Company
London, 1985

Stepaniak, Joanne and Kathy
Hecker
*Ecological Cooking: Recipes to
Save the Planet*
The Book Publishing Company
Summertown, Tenn., 1991

Stepaniak, Joanne
*Table for Two: Meat- and Dairy-
Free Recipes for Two*
The Book Publishing Company
Summertown, Tenn., 1996

Stepaniak, Joanne
The Uncheese Cookbook
The Book Publishing Company
Summertown, Tenn., 1994

Stepaniak, Joanne
*Vegan Vittles: A Collection of
Recipes Inspired by the Critters of
Farm Sanctuary*
The Book Publishing Company
Summertown, Tenn., 1996

Wasserman, Debra
*Simply Vegan: Quick Vegetarian
Meals*
The Vegetarian Resource Group
Baltimore, Md., 1991

REFERENCE BOOKS

Akers, Keith
*A Vegetarian Sourcebook: The
Nutrition, Ecology, and Ethics of a
Natural Foods Diet*
Vegetarian Press
Denver, Colo., 1983, 1989

Barnard, Neal, M.D.
Eat Right, Live Longer
Harmony Books
New York, 1995

Barnard, Neal, M.D.
Food For Life
Crown Publishers, Inc.
New York, 1993

Barnard, Neal, M.D.
*Foods That Cause You to Lose
Weight: The Negative Calorie
Effect*
The Book Publishing Company
Summertown, Tenn., 1992

Barnard, Neal, M.D.
The Power of Your Plate: A Plan for Better Living
Book Publishing Company
Summertown, Tenn., 1990

Coats, C. David
Old MacDonald's Factory Farm
Continuum Publishing Co.
New York, 1989

Davis, Karen
Prisoned Chickens, Poisoned Eggs: An Inside Look at the Modern Poultry Industry
Book Publishing Company
Summertown, Tenn., 1996

Fox, Michael W., D.V.M.
Farm Animals: Husbandry, Behavior, and Veterinary Practices
University Park Press
Baltimore, Md., 1984

Gabbe, David A.
Why Do Vegetarians Eat Like That? Everything You Wanted to Know (and Some Things You Didn't) About Vegetarianism
Prime Imprints, Ltd.
Eugene, Ore., 1994

Gold, Mark
Assault and Battery: What Factory Farming Means for Humans and Animals
Pluto Press Ltd.
London, 1983

Iacobbo, Karen and Michael Edward Gibson
Vegetarian Magic in Three Easy Steps: Change Your Mind, Change the Menu
American Lyceum Publishing
Providence, R.I., 1996

Klaper, Michael, M.D.
Pregnancy, Children and the Vegan Diet
Gentle World, Inc.
Umatilla, Fla., 1987

Klaper, Michael, M.D.
Vegan Nutrition: Pure and Simple
Gentle World, Inc.
Umatilla, Fla., 1987

Mason, Jim and Peter Singer
Animal Factories
Crown Publishers
New York, 1980

McDougall, John A., M.D., and Mary A. McDougall
The McDougall Plan
New Century Publishers, Inc.
Piscataway, N.J., 1983

Messina, Virginia and Mark Messina
The Vegetarian Way: Total Health for You and Your Family
Crown Trade Paperbacks
New York, 1996

Rifkin, Jeremy
Beyond Beef: The Rise and Fall of the Cattle Culture
Plume, a division of Penguin Books
New York, 1993

Robbins, John
Diet for a New America
Stillpoint Publishing
Walpole, N.H., 1987

Robbins, John
May All Be Fed
Avon Books
New York, 1992

Singer, Peter
Animal Liberation
Random House, Inc.
New York, 1990

Wasserman, Debra and Reed Mangels, Ph.D., R.D.
Vegan Handbook
The Vegetarian Resource Group
Baltimore, Md., 1996

Yntema, Sharon
Vegetarian Baby: A Complete and Valuable Source Book for Vegetarian Parents
McBooks Press
Ithaca, N.Y., 1980, 1984, 1991

Yntema, Sharon
Vegetarian Children: A Supportive Guide for Parents
McBooks Press
Ithaca, N.Y., 1987

MAGAZINES

Vegetarian Journal
P.O. Box 1463
Baltimore, MD 21203-1463
Tel.: 410-366-8343

Vegetarian Times
P.O. Box 570
Oak Park, IL 60303-0570
Tel.: 708-848-8100
Fax: 708-848-8175

Veggie Life
1041 Shary Cir.
Concord, CA 94518-2407
Tel.: 510-671-9852
Fax: 510-671-0692

Vegetarian Voice
P.O. Box 72
Dolgeville, NY 13329-0072
Tel.: 518-736-4686

WORLD WIDE WEB SITES

The Internet holds a wealth of information on vegetarianism, but site addresses often change. The best way to find current sites that contain the information you're looking for is to do a search. But here are a few to get you started:

http://www.cyber-kitchen.com/pgvegtar.htm
A list of many vegetarian recipe resources on the Web.
Part of the Cyber Kitchen site.

http://www.vegkitchen.com/
The Vegetarian Kitchen is the Web site of cookbook author Nava Atlas.
Includes great recipes and tips.

http://mastermall.com/vegan/gourmet/
Gourmet vegetarian recipe archives. Lots and lots of recipes.

http://www.fatfree.com/
The low-fat vegetarian recipe archives.

http://www.veg.org/veg/Orgs/VegSocUK/Recipes/recindx.html
Recipes from the U.K. Vegetarian Society.

http://www.babyville.com/gkc/
Good Karma Cafe.

http://www.vegweb.com/
Veggies Unite site—recipes, tips, animal rights, etc.

http://www.vegetariantimes.com
Vegetarian Times, Web site.

http://www.veg.org/veg/
Vegetarian guide. Links to many recipes and other veg sites.

http://www.peta-online.org
PETA's Web site.

INDEX

Agar 207
Aioli 23
Almond Tarts 171
Almond-Walnut-Zucchini Loaf 127
Amazing Apple and Date Mousse 190
Appetizer Rolls 51-54
Appetizer tips 40
Apple
  and Date Mousse, Amazing 190
  Cake, Awesome 168
  Maple Muffins 158
  Streusel Pie, The Best 173
Arborio rice 207
Arrowroot 207
Artichoke
  Hearts With Fresh Basil 74
  Tofu Pasta 106
Asian Pasta 74
Awesome Apple Cake 168

Bacon, Better Than 32
"Bacon"-Orange Dressing, Creamy 90
Balsamic vinegar
  about 207
  Mushroom Salad with 81
Bananas
  Cocoa Muffins 159
  Crispy Wrapped Baked 194
  French Toast 35
  Juicy Jungle Punch 204
Barbecue
  Beans and Smoky Spuds 131
  No-Blues 100
Barley
  about 207
  Mushroom Soup 69
Bars
  Chocolate Chip Brownie 182
  Peanut Better 188
  Raspberry Crumble 189
Basil, Fresh, With Artichoke Hearts 74
Bean sprouts 207
"Beat the Heat" Bulgur Salad 75
Beef
  about 13
  "Beefless" Stew 107
  Beefy Seitan Roast 108
Beets
  Classic Borshch 58
Berry Medley Pie 172
Better Bread Spread 165
Better Than Bacon 32
Bisque, Creamy Tomato 66
Black Beans
  Chili, Bodacious 63
  Feijoada 140
  Smoky Spuds and BBQ Beans 131

Bleu "Cheese" Salad Dressing 89
Blueberry
  "Cheese" Cake 174
  Muffins, Very 164
Bobbi's Blissful Chocolate-Rum Pie 175
Bodacious Black Bean Chili 63
Books, vegetarian 214-215
Borshch, Classic 58
Bowtie Surprise With Grilled Garden
    Veggies 76
Brandy
  Eggless "Eggnog" 203
  Orange Sauce 195
Breads
  Challah 156
  Corn, Incredible 161
  Lemon Poppy Seed 162
  Piña Colada 163
  Super Soy 157
Breakfast Casserole 28
Brownie Bars, Chocolate Chip 182
Brown rice syrup 207
Brown rice vinegar 207
Bulgur
  about 207
  Salad 75
Burritos, Funny-Face 118
Butterbean, Butterbean Pâté 41
Butternut and Chestnut Holiday Sauté
    109

Cabbage
  Thai Cole Slaw 88
Cajun-Style "Fish Cakes" 115
Cake
  Apple, Awesome 168
  Blueberry "Cheese" 174
  "Cream"-Filled Orange Crumb 169
  Pumpkin Spice 170
Capers 207
Carob 207
Carob-Peanut Butter Smoothie 200
Carrots, Glazed 152
Cashew butter 207
Casserole, Breakfast 28
Celery Soup, Incredible Cream of 70
Challah 156
"Cheese"
  Bleu, Salad Dressing 89
  Blueberry Cake 174
  Melty Pizza 19
Chestnut and Butternut Holiday Sauté
    109
Chick-Peas
  Curry 111
  Hummus 45
  Pita Pockets 96
  Taste of Morocco 136

Chicken
  about 14
  Friendly Tofu Nuggets With Maple-
    Mustard Dipping Sauce 110
  Mock, Salad 80
  Un-, Fillet 104
Chili, Bodacious Black Bean 63
Chili, White 71
Chipotle chilies
  about 207
  Chipotle Split Pea Soup 64
  Linguine With Smoky Tomato Sauce 144
Chives
  and Margarine Spread 165
  and Mashed Potatoes 146
Chocolate
  Chocolate Chip Brownie Bars 182
  Chocolate Chip Cookies 183
  Fudgy Cocoa Mint Cookies 185
  Mexican-Style Hot Chocolate 202
  "Nice Cream" 196
  Peanut Better Bars 188
  Peanut Butter Perfection,
    Karen's 177
  Pudding 191
  Rum Pie, Bobbi's Blissful 175
Cilantro 208
Classic Borshch 58
Cocoa
  -Banana Muffins 159
  Mint Cookies, Fudgy 185
Coconut
  Flan 192
  milk 208
Cole Slaw Dressing, Easy 23
Cole Slaw, Thai 88
Comforting Knishes 112
Cookies
  Chocolate Chip 183
  Fudgy Cocoa Mint 185
  Oatmeal 187
Corn Bread, Incredible 161
Couscous
  about 208
  Summery Stuffed Peppers 134
  Taste of Morocco 136
Cranberry Salad 77
"Cream Cheese"
  Roasted Red Pepper 166
  Soy-Free 20
  Spread, Tofu 21
"Cream"-Filled Orange Crumb Cake 169
Cream, Sweet Topping 24
Creamy
  "Bacon"-Orange Dressing 90
  Chive Mashed Potatoes 146
  Country Gravy 38
  Dill Dressing 91
  Potato Leek Soup 65
  Tomato Bisque 66

Crêpes, Simply Superb 30
Crispy
    Rice Treats 184
    Tofu Cubes 94, 113
    Wrapped Baked Bananas 194
Crostini, Elegant Eggplant 49
Crumb Cake, "Cream"-Filled Orange 169
Cucumbers, Sweet and Sour 86
Curried Dip 43
Curry, Chick-Pea 111
Curry paste 208

Dairy-free alternatives 10
Dal Soup, Delectable 67
Danish
    Decidedly Delicious 160
    Prune 161
Date and Apple Mousse,
    Amazing 190
Decidedly Delicious Danish 160
Delectable Dal Soup 67
Dessert shortcuts, easy 176
Deviled Tempeh Spread 97
Dill Dressing, Creamy 91
Dips
    Curried 43
    Fiesta 43
    Fiesta Lite 43
    Maple-Mustard Dipping Sauce 110
    Onion 46
    Pesto 47
Dressings
    Bleu "Cheese" 89
    Creamy "Bacon"-Orange 90
    Creamy Dill 91
    Easy Cole Slaw 23
    Fat-Free Salad Slimmer 92
    Poppy Seed Passion 92
    Sensational "Soy-onnaise" 93
    Terrific Tartar Sauce 94
    Thousand Island 94
    Tofu Tartar Sauce 23
Dried Tomatoes, Wine-Marinated 56

Easy Cole Slaw Dressing 23
Easy dessert Shortcuts 176
Easy Pumpkin Pie 176
Egg-free mayonnaise 208
Eggless
    "Eggnog" 203
    "Egg" Wash 156
"Eggnog," Eggless 203
Eggplant
    Crostini, Elegant 49
    Moussaka 124
    Sandwich, Italian 98
Egg replacer 10, 208
Elegant Eggplant Crostini 49
Erica's Wonderful Waffles 36

Fabulous Fatoosh 78
Fajitas, Fire-Up-the-Grill 116
Fake Feta, Frankly 22
Fat-Free Salad Slimmer 92
Fatoosh, Fabulous 78
Faux Fish Cakes 94, 114-15
Feijoada, Vegetarian 140
Feta, Frankly Fake 22
Fiesta Dip 43
Filet, Un-Chicken 104
Filling appetizer rolls 54
Filling, Key Lime Pie 178
Fire-Up-the Grill-Fajitas 116
Fish, about 14
Fish Cakes , Faux 114-115
Flan, Coconut 192
Focaccia, Fragrant 50
Fragrant Focaccia 50
Frankly Fake Feta 22, 79
French-Fried Onion String
    Beans 146
French Toast
    Banana 35
    Royale 35
Fresh Shiitake Pâté 42
Fruit
    Drink, Lassi 201
    Pie, Tutti Fruity 181
    Smoothie 200
    Smoothie, Taste of The Tropics 205
    Tarts, Minced 180
Fudgy Cocoa Mint Cookies 185
Funny-Face Burritos 118

Garlic Stuffed Potatoes 147
Gentle Shepherd's Pie 119
Gingerroot 208
Ginger Sauce 132
Glazed Root Vegetables 152
Gluten flour, instant 208
Golden Vegetable Noodle Soup 59
Gravy
    Creamy Country 38
    Mushroom 137
Great Greek Salad 79
Greek Salad, Great 79
Green Beans
    and French-Fried Onions 146
    Stroganoff 153
Grilling tips 117
Guacamole, Holy Moly 44

Hash Browns, Homestyle 37
Hearty Winter Squash-and-Potato
    Soup 68
Herbed Olive Spread 44
"Hollandaise," Tofu 23
Holy Moly Guacamole 44, 60

Homestyle Hash Browns 37
Hot and Spicy Lo Mein 120, 192
Hot Chocolate, Mexican-Style 202
Hot-Shot Soup 60
Hummus 45

Ice Cream, Nondairy
    Chocolate "Nice Cream" 196
    Strawberry "Nice Cream" 197
Incredible Corn Bread 161
Incredible Cream of Celery Soup 70
Indian Samosas, Savory 52
Indian-Style "Fish Cakes" 115
Instant gluten flour 208
Italian
    Eggplant Sandwich 98
    Sausage, Mock 33

Jamaican Stuffed Pastries 51
Jamaican-Style "Fish Cakes" 115
Jean's Pecan Balls 186
Jerk Tempeh or Tofu 121
Jicama
    about 208
    Salad With Orange Vinaigrette 80
Juicy Jungle Punch 204

Kalamata olives 208
Karen's Chocolate-Peanut Butter
    Perfection 177
Kebabs, Lucky Luau 122
Kelp 208
Key Lime Pie Filling 178
Knishes, Comforting 112
Kombu 208
Kugel, Savory Noodle 145

Lasagne, Magnificent "Meaty" 123
Lassi 201
Leek Potato Soup, Creamy 65
Leeks 208
Lemon
    Pie, Luscious 179
    Poppy Seed Bread 162
Lime
    Key Lime Pie Filling 178
    Strawberry Freeze 204
Linguine With Smoky Tomato Sauce 144
Liquid smoke 208
Lite Fiesta Dip 43
Loaf
    Neat 126
    Nutty Zucchini 127
Lo Mein, Hot and Spicy 120
Lucky Luau Kebabs 122
Luscious Lemon Pie 179

Magazines, vegetarian 215
Magnificent "Meaty" Lasagne 123

Magnificent Minestrone 61
Maple
  -Apple Muffins 158
  -Mustard Dipping Sauce 110
Marinade, Marvelous 149, 152
Marinara Madness 18, 101, 123
Marmite 209
Marvelous Marinade 149, 152
Mayonnaise, Tofu 23
Meat substitutes 8
"Meaty"
  Lasagne, Magnificent 123
  Mushroom Sandwiches 99
Melty Pizza "Cheese" 19
"Meringue" Topping 179
Mexican-Style Hot Chocolate 202
Milk, about 15
Minced Fruit Tarts 180
Minestrone, Magnificent 61
Mint, Fudgy Cocoa Cookies 185
Mirin 209
Miso 209
Mock
  Chicken Salad 80
  Italian Sausage 33
  Sausage 33
Moussaka 124
Mousse, Amazing Apple and Date 190
Muffins
  Apple-Maple 158
  Blueberry, Very 164
  Cocoa-Banana 159
Mung Beans
  about 209
  Soup 67
Mushrooms
  about 209
  Barley Soup 69
  Fresh Shiitake Pâté 42
  Gravy 137
  Portobellos, Sherried 130
  Quick Stroganoff 128
  Salad With Balsamic Vinegar 81
  Sandwiches, "Meaty" 99

Neat Loaf 126
No-Blues BBQ 100
Noodel Kugel, Savory 145
Noodles
  Soup, Golden Vegetable 59
  Szechuan 135
  With Peanut Sauce 82
Nouveau Sloppy Joe 101
Nutritional yeast 209
Nuts, Thrice as Nice Spiced 55
Nuttin' Butter Spread 165
Nutty Zucchini Loaf 127

Oat flour 209
Oatmeal Cookies 187
Oil substitute for dressings 92
Olde-Fashioned Plum Pudding 195
Olive Spread, Herbed 44
Onion
  Dip 46
  French-Fried Onion String Beans 146
  Soup, Thick and Creamy 62
Orange
  Brandy Sauce 195
  Crumb Cake, "Cream"-Filled 169
  Dressing, Creamy "Bacon" 90
  Vinaigrette, With Jicama Salad 80

Pancakes, Wake- 'Em-Up 34
Papa Pedro's Potato Salad 83
Parsnips, Glazed 152
Pasta
  Artichoke Tofu 106
  Asian 74
  Golden Vegetable Noodle Soup 59
  Linguine With Smoky Tomato Sauce 144
  Noodles With Peanut Sauce 82
  Savory Noodel Kugel 145
  Szechuan Noodles 135
Pasta Salad
  Bowtie Surprise With Grilled Garden Veggies 76
  Psychedelic 84
  With Peanut Sauce 82
Pastries, Stuffed Jamaican 51
Pâté
  Butterbean, Butterbean 41
  Shiitake, Fresh 42
Patties, Rice 102
Peanuts
  Better Bars 188
  Butter-Carob Smoothie 200
  Butter-Chocolate Perfection, Karen's 177
  Sauce, Noodles With 82
Pecan Balls, Jean's 186
Pepperoncinis 43, 209
Peppers
  "Cream Cheese," Roasted 166
  Stuffed Roasted Poblanos 133
  Stuffed With Polenta and Tomatoes 151
  Stuffed With Zucchini and Tomatoes 151
  Summery Stuffed 134
Pesto Dip 47
Phyllo pastry
  about 209
  Crispy Wrapped Baked Bananas 194
  Filling Appetizer Rolls 54
  Jamaican Stuffed Pastries 51
  Savory Indian Samosas 52
  Spanikopita Rolls 53

Pie
  Apple Streusel, The Best 173
  Berry Medley 172
  Chocolate-Peanut Butter Perfection, Karen's 177
  Chocolate-Rum, Bobbi's Blissful 175
  Filling, Key Lime 178
  Lemon, Luscious 179
  Pumpkin, Easy 176
  Tutti Fruity 181
Piña Colada Bread 163
Pine nuts 209
Pinto Bean, Burritos 118
Pita Pockets With Chick-Peas 96
Pizza
  "Cheese," Melty 19
  Roasted Veggie 129
  Tips 129
Plum Pudding, Olde-Fashioned 195
Poblano peppers
  about 209
  Roasted and Stuffed 133
Polenta
  and Tomato Stuffed Peppers 151
  With Zucchini and Tomatoes 151
Popeye's Delight 148
Poppy Seed
  Lemon Bread 162
  Passion Dressing 92
Pork, about 15
Portobellos, Sherried 130
Potatoes
  Breakfast Casserole 28
  Challah 156
  Comforting Knishes 112
  Creamy Chive Mashed Potatoes 146
  Garlic Stuffed 147
  Hash Browns, Homestyle 37
  Hearty Winter Squash-and-Potato Soup 68
  Knishes, Comforting 112
  Leek Soup, Creamy 65
  Popeye's Delight 148
  Roasted, with Rosemary 149
  Salad, Papa Pedro's 83
  Salad, Red-Skin 85
  Shepherd's Pie, Gentle 119
Prune Danish 161
Psychedelic Pasta Salad 84
Pudding
  Chocolate 191
  Coconut Flan 192
  Plum, Olde-Fashioned 195
Pumpkin
  Pie, Easy 176
  Spice Cake 170
Punch, Juicy Jungle 204

Quick Stroganoff 128

Raisins
  Minced Fruit Tarts 180
Raspberry Crumble Bars 189
Really Easy Risotto 150
Red-Skin Potato Salad 85
Reference books, vegetarian 214-15
Resources, vegetarian 212-16
Rice
  Patties 102
  Risotto, Really Easy 150
  Treats, Crispy 184
  wine vinegar 209
Risotto, Really Easy 150
Roast, Beefy Seitan 108
Roasted
  Pepper "Cream Cheese" 166
  Poblanos, Stuffed 133
  Rosemary Potatoes 149
  Veggie Pizza 129
Rolls
  Appetizer 51-54
  Spanikopita 53
Roll-Ups, Tex-Mex, Tortilla 103
Root Vegetables, Glazed 152
Rosemary with Roasted Potatoes 149
Rum-Chocolate Pie, Bobbi's Blissful 175
Rutabaga 209

Salads
  Artichoke Hearts With Fresh Basil 74
  Asian Pasta 74
  "Beat the Heat" Bulgur 75
  Bowtie Surprise With Grilled Garden
    Veggies 76
  Cranberry 77
  Fabulous Fatoosh 78
  Great Greek 79
  Jicama Salad With Orange Vinaigrette
    80
  Mock Chicken 80
  Mushroom Salad With Balsamic
    Vinegar 81
  Noodles With Peanut Sauce 82
  Papa Pedro's Potato 83
  Psychedelic Pasta 84
  Red-Skin Potato 85
  Sweet-and-Sour Cukes 86
  Tasty "Toona" 87
  Thai Cole Slaw 88
Salsa Cups, South-of-the-Border 48
Samosas, Savory Indian 52
Sandwiches
  Chick-Pea Pita Pockets 96
  Deviled Tempeh Spread 97
  Italian Eggplant 98
  "Meaty" Mushroom 100
  No-Blues BBQ 99

Sandwiches (continued)
  Nouveau Sloppy Joe 101
  Rice Patties 102
  Tex-Mex Tortilla Roll-Ups 103
  tips 97
  Un-Chicken Filet 104
Sauces
  Ginger 132
  Maple-Mustard, Dipping 110
  Marinara Madness 18
  Orange Brandy 195
  Peanut, With Noodles 82
  Tangy Cream 124
  Tomato, Smoky 144
  Worcestershire, Veggie 25
Sausage, Mock 33
Sausage, Mock Italian 33
Savory Indian Samosas 52
Savory Noodel Kugel 145
Scotch bonnet peppers 210
Scramble-icious ideas 29
Scrambles, Southwest 29
Seitan
  about 210
  Quick Stroganoff 128
  Roast, Beefy 108
Sensational "Soy-onnaise" Dressing 93
Sesame meal 210
Sesame oil 210
Shallots 210
Shepherd's Pie, Gentle 119
Sherried Portobellos 130
Shiitake Pâté, Fresh 42
Simply Superb Crêpes 30
Sloppy Joe, Nouveau 101
Smoky Spuds and BBQ Beans 131
Smoothies
  Carob-Peanut Butter 200
  Fruit 200
  Taste of the Tropics 205
Soba noodles 210
Soups, creamy
  Incredible Cream of Celery Soup 70
  Potato Leek Soup 65
  Thick and Creamy Onion Soup 62
  Tomato Bisque 66
Soups, hearty
  Bodacious Black Bean Chili 63
  Chipotle Split Pea 64
  Delectable Dal 67
  Hearty Winter Squash-and-Potato 68
  Mushroom Barley 69
  White Chili 71
Soups, vegetable broth
  Classic Borshch 58
  Golden Vegetable Noodle 59
  Hot-Shot 60
  Magnificent Minestrone 61

Sour Cream, Tofu 24
South-of-the-Border Salsa Cups 48
Southwest Scrambles 29, 30
Soy Bread, Super 157
Soy Flour
  about 210
  Crêpes, Simply Superb 30
  Super Soy Bread 157
Soy-Free Cream Cheese 20
Soymilk
  about 210
  "Cream"-Filled Orange Crumb Cake
    169
  Eggless "Eggnog" 203
  Key Lime Pie Filling 178
  powder 210
  Super Soy Bread 157
"Soy-onnaise" Dressing, Sensational 93
Spanikopita Rolls 53
Spice Cake, Pumpkin 170
Spiced Nuts, Thrice As Nice 55
Spinach
  Popeye's Delight 148
Split Peas
  Golden Vegetable Noodle Soup 59
  Split Pea Chipotle Soup 64
Spreads
  Better Bread 165
  Deviled Tempeh 97
  Herbed Olive 44
  Nuttin' Butter 165
  Tofu Cream Cheese 21
Squash-and-Potato Soup, Hearty Winter
    68
Stew, "Beefless" 107
Sticks, Tempting Tempeh 31
Stir-Fried Tofu and Vegetables in Ginger
    Sauce 132
Strawberry
  Lime Freeze 204
  "Nice Cream" 197
String Beans, French-Fried Onion 146
Stroganoff
  Green Bean 153
  Quick 128
Stuffed
  Jamaican Pastries 51
  Peppers, Polenta and Tomato 151
  Peppers, Summery 134
  Potatoes, Garlic 147
  Roasted Poblanos 133
Summery Stuffed Peppers 134
Super Soy Bread 157
Sweet-and-Sour
  Cukes 86
  Vegetables 154
Sweet Cream Topping 24

Sweet Potatoes
Smoky Spuds and BBQ Beans 131
Szechuan hot bean paste 210
Szechuan Noodles 135, 192
Tahini 210
Tamari 210
Tangy Cream Sauce 124
Tapioca 210
Tartar Sauce
Terrific Tartar Sauce 94
Tofu Tartar Sauce 23
Tarts
Almond 171
Minced Fruit 180
Taste of Morocco 136
Taste of the Tropics Smoothie 205
Tasty "Toona" Salad 87
Tempeh
about 8, 210
Deviled Spread 97
Jerk 121
Kebabs, Lucky Luau 122
Sloppy Joes 101
Sticks, Tempting 31
Tempting Tempeh Sticks 31
Terrific Tartar Sauce 94
Tex-Mex Tortilla Roll-Ups 103
Textured vegetable protein
about 210
"Beefless" Stew 107
Bodacious Black Bean Chili 63
Lasagne, Magnificent "Meaty" 123
Moussaka 124
Pastries, Stuffed Jamaican 51
Sausage, mock 33
Thai
Cole Slaw 88
"Fish Cakes" 115
red chili paste 210
The Best Apple Streusel Pie 173
Thick and Creamy Onion Soup 62
Thousand Island Dressing 94
Thrice As Nice Spiced Nuts 55
Toast, French Royale 35
Tofu
about 9, 211
Aioli 23
Better Than Bacon 32
Bleu "Cheese" Salad Dressing 89
Chicken-Friendly Nuggets With Maple-
Mustard Dipping Sauce 110
Chocolate Chip Brownie Bars 182
Chocolate "Nice Cream" 196
Chocolate Pudding 191
Chocolate-Rum Pie, Bobbi's Blissful 175
Cream Cheese Spread 21
"Cream"-Filled Orange Crumb Cake
169

Tofu (continued)
Creamy "Bacon"-Orange Dressing 90
Creamy Dill Dressing 91
Creamy Potato Leek Soup 65
Creamy Tomato Bisque 66
Crispy Cubes 113
Curried Dip 43
Danish 160
Easy Cole Slaw Dressing 23
Eggless "Eggnog" 203
Fajitas 116
Faux Fish Cakes 114
Feta, Frankly Fake 22
Filet, Un-Chicken 104
Foo Young 137
freezing 9
Greek Salad 79
Green Bean Stroganoff 153
"Hollandaise" 23
Jerk 121
Karen's Chocolate-Peanut Butter
Perfection 177
Lasagne, Magnificent "Meaty" 123
Loaf, Neat 126
Lo Mein, Hot and Spicy 120
Mayonnaise 23, 90
Minestrone 61
Mock Chicken Salad 80
No-Blues BBQ 100
Not-a-Turkey 138, 146
Onion Dip 46
Pasta, Artichoke 106
Roasted Pepper "Cream Cheese"
166
Savory Noodel Kugel 145
Scramble-icious, ideas 29
Sour Cream 24, 80, 128
Southwest Scrambles 29
Sensational "Soy-onnaise" Dressing
93
Stir-Fried Vegetables in Ginger
Sauce 132
Strawberry "Nice Cream" 197
Stuffed Roasted Poblanos 133
Tartar Sauce 23, 94
Taste of the Tropics Smoothie 205
Tasty "Toona" Salad 87
Topping, Sweet Cream 24
Zucchini Boats 141
Tomatoes
Bisque, Creamy 66
Fatoosh 78
Linguine With Smoky Tomato Sauce
144
Polenta With Zucchini and 164
Stuffed Peppers, Polenta and 164
Wine-Marinated, Dried 56

Topping
"Meringue" 179
Sweet Cream 24
Tortilla Roll-Ups, Tex-Mex 103
Turkey
about 14
Tofu Not-a-Turkey 138
Turnips, Glazed 152
Tutti Fruity Pie 181

Udon noodles 211
Ume (or umeboshi) plum vinegar 211
Un-Chicken Filet 94, 104

Vegan cheese 211
Vegetable
bouillon cubes 211
broth 211
broth powder 211
Vegetarian
children, feeding 11
cookbooks 214
Feijoada 140
food resources 212
groups 213
magazines 215
"meats" 211
reference books 214
Vegetarianism and health 13
Veggie Worcestershire Sauce 25, 60, 145
211
Very Blueberry Muffins 174
Vinaigrette, Orange, With Jicama Salad
80
Vinegar, Mushroom Salad With Balsamic
81
Vital wheat gluten 211

Waffles, Erica's Wonderful 36
Wake-'Em-Up Pancakes 34
Walnut-Almond-Zucchini Loaf 127
Warm Winter Wine 206
Web sites, vegetarian 216
White Chili 71
Wine
Marinated Dried Tomatoes 56
Warm Winter 206
Worcestershire Sauce, Veggie 25, 211

Zucchini
and Tomatoes, Polenta 151
Boats 141
Fudgy Cocoa Mint Cookies 185
Loaf, Nutty 127

Cooking With PETA features many delicious, kind-to-animals recipes from best-selling authors Bryanna Clark Grogan and Louise Hagler.

If you're looking to add more variety to your menus or want to learn more about cooking without meat, eggs, or dairy products, pick up these popular cookbooks today!

By Louise Hagler

Tofu
Quick & Easy,
revised
$11.95

Lighten Up!
$11.95

Soyfoods
Cookery
$9.95

Tofu Cookery
$16.95

By Bryanna Clark Grogan

20 Minutes to
Dinner
$12.95

The (Almost) No Fat
Cookbook
$12.95

The (Almost) No Fat
Holiday Cookbook
$12.95

Available in bookstores, or you can order your copy today by calling:
1-800-695-2241